Afghanistan to Latvia – see inside back cover for Leba

PHILIP'S

Early Years Atlas

DAVID WRIGHT AND RACHEL NOONAN

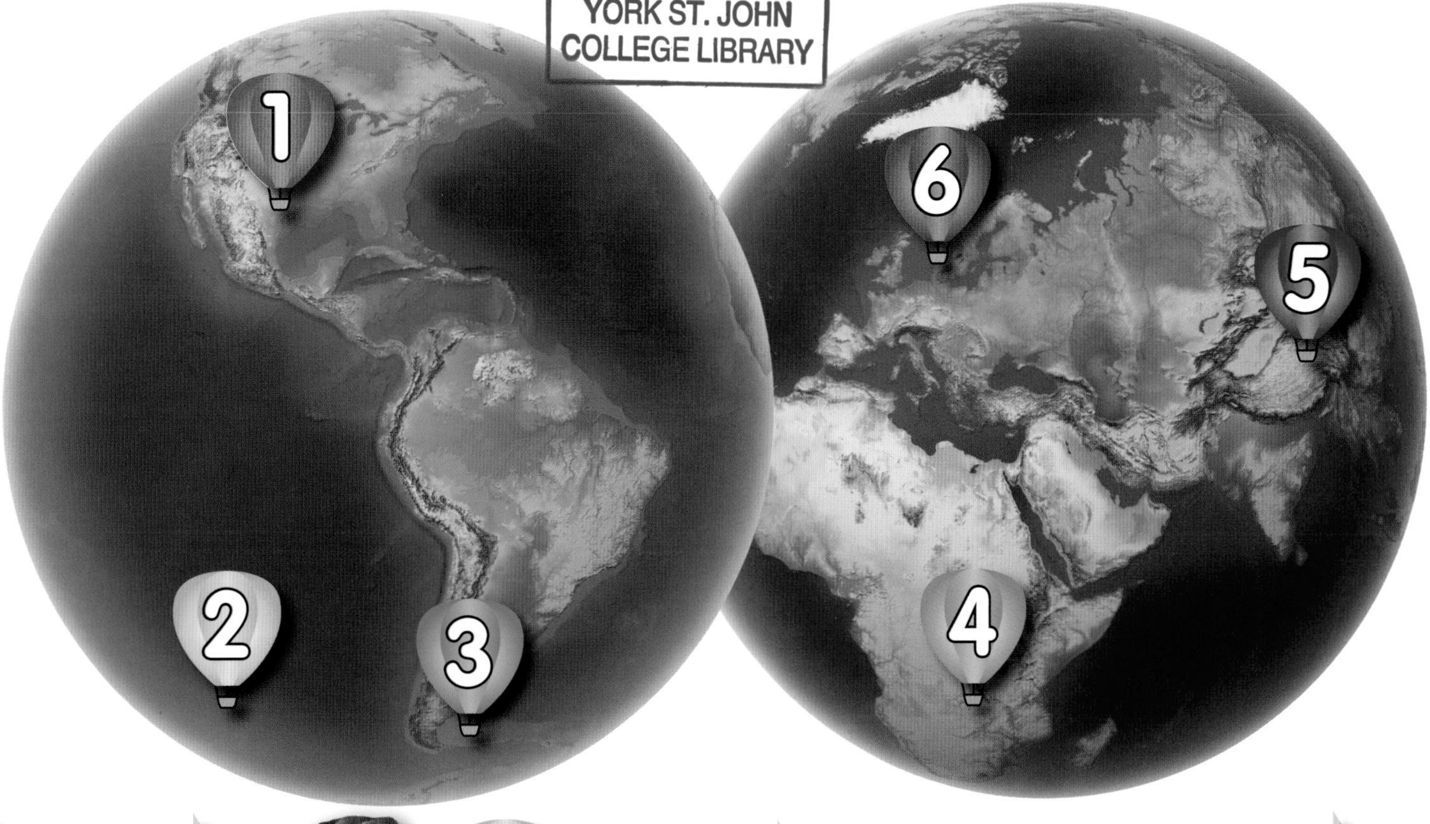

1 **Buffalo live here!** page 41

2 **Huge statues are here!** page 35

3 **There are cowboys here!** page 45

4 **Gorillas live here!** page 32

5 **The longest wall is here!** page 28

6 **Snowy owls live here!** page 15

About this Atlas

Ideas for grown-ups

Young children are constantly expanding their knowledge and understanding of the world. This innovative atlas gives lots of opportunities to enjoy making discoveries....

- ★ Enjoy a voyage of discovery together with a book designed for sharing. So dip in and out again and again!
- ★ The '**hot air balloon**' takes children to real, exciting places and the real location can be found on the map.
- ★ The words are mostly for adults to read to children, but the first sentence is bigger and simpler so that they can 'have a go' as they begin to develop reading skills.
- ★ Young children enjoy learning through discovery so there are interactive '**Can you**' activities for you to try together! You will also find '**Ideas for grown-ups**' boxes with extra ideas for you to talk about and look at with the children.
- ★ It's a wonderful world – this atlas is designed to help your wonderful children enjoy discovering more about our world.

When you've enjoyed this atlas, why not take a look at *Philip's Infant School Atlas* for 5–7 year olds and *Philip's Children's Atlas* for 7–12 year olds.

Message to Children

(Adults – please read to them!)

This atlas is for you! We can't tell you everything about the whole world, but we can take you to some exciting places, so jump into our hot air balloon and let's explore! Choose a page, look at the pictures and find the real places on the map. Then choose another page and explore new places.

Who are the Authors?

David Wright

David Wright has enjoyed visiting 106 countries, to bring first-hand experience to this atlas. He has been both a teacher and a teacher trainer, as well as a university lecturer in Norwich, UK.

Rachel Noonan

Rachel Noonan is a graduate of the Open University. She has travelled right round the world and works with young children in a primary school in Norwich. This atlas is dedicated to her 3 children.

First published in Great Britain in 2009 by Philip's,
a division of Octopus Publishing Group Limited
www.octopusbooks.co.uk
2–4 Heron Quays, London E14 4JP
An Hachette UK Company
www.hachettelivre.co.uk

To Florence, Molly and Isaac

Cartography by Philip's

A CIP catalogue record for this book is available from the British Library.

ISBN 978-0-540-09120-1

Printed in Hong Kong

Details of other Philip's titles and services can be found on our website at: **www.philips-maps.co.uk**

Contents

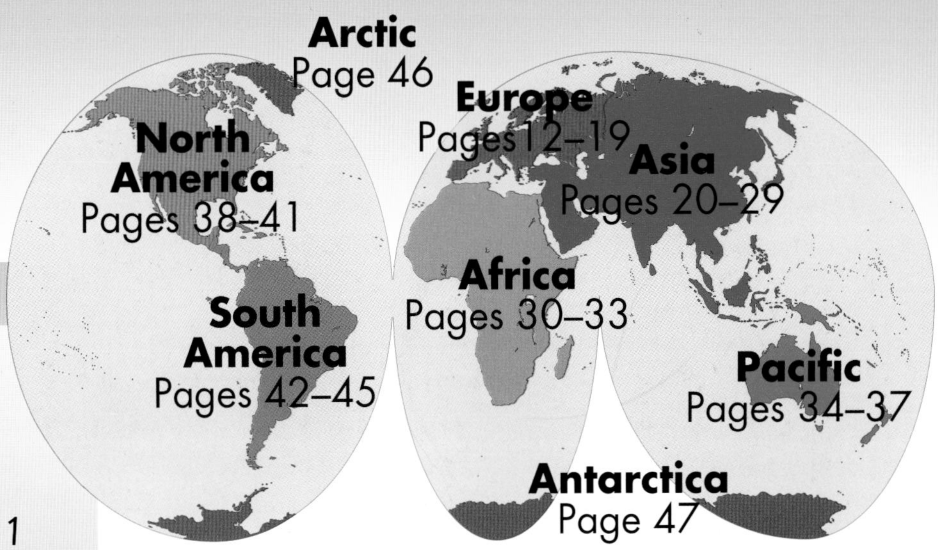
Arctic
Page 46
Europe
Pages 12–19
North
America
Pages 38–41
Asia
Pages 20–29
Africa
Pages 30–33
South
America
Pages 42–45
Pacific
Pages 34–37
Antarctica
Page 47

Philip's and the Royal Geographical Society

This Philip's atlas displays the logo of the **Royal Geographical Society** (with the **Institute of British Geographers**). The Royal Geographical Society supports education, teaching, research and expeditions. The role of 'promoting public understanding of geography' now reaches 3 to 5 year olds through this new atlas.

Philip's has been publishing good maps for over 150 years.

Find out more about the Royal Geographical Society! Visit their website at www.rgs.org – David Wright is a Fellow and a Chartered Geographer of the RGS.

Our Planet in Space

Let's jump into a space ship!

Our planet Earth is one of **8 planets** that orbit (go round) our Sun. Can you count 8 planets?

Big and small planets.

Can you see

2 big planets?

J______ and S_____

2 middle sized planets?

U_____ and N______

4 small planets?

M______, V____, E____ and M___

Which planet do you think is the **biggest**?
Which planet do you think is the **smallest**?

Look at the stars.

They are all other suns even further away from Earth than Neptune!

Near and far. Hot and cold.

The planets in our Solar System all go round our Sun.
Mercury is near the Sun. Do you think it is very **hot** or very cold?
Neptune is far away from the Sun. Is it very **cold** or very hot?

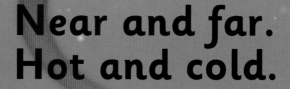

What shape are the planets?

Did you know that all the planets are spheres (the same shape as a ball)? Can you find a planet with rings around it? It is **Saturn**.

Ideas for grown-ups

Look at the diagram with the children and see if they can work out the answers to the questions themselves.

★ Play with some balls to feel the shapes and sizes of the planets – use big balls and small balls.

★ Try: a basketball (Jupiter), a soccer ball (Saturn), 2 softballs (Uranus, Neptune), 2 Ping Pong balls (Earth, Venus), a big marble (Mars), a small marble (Mercury).

★ And don't forget to look at the stars! There are so many! Think how small the world is and yet how big it is when you walk or drive – or even fly in an aeroplane.

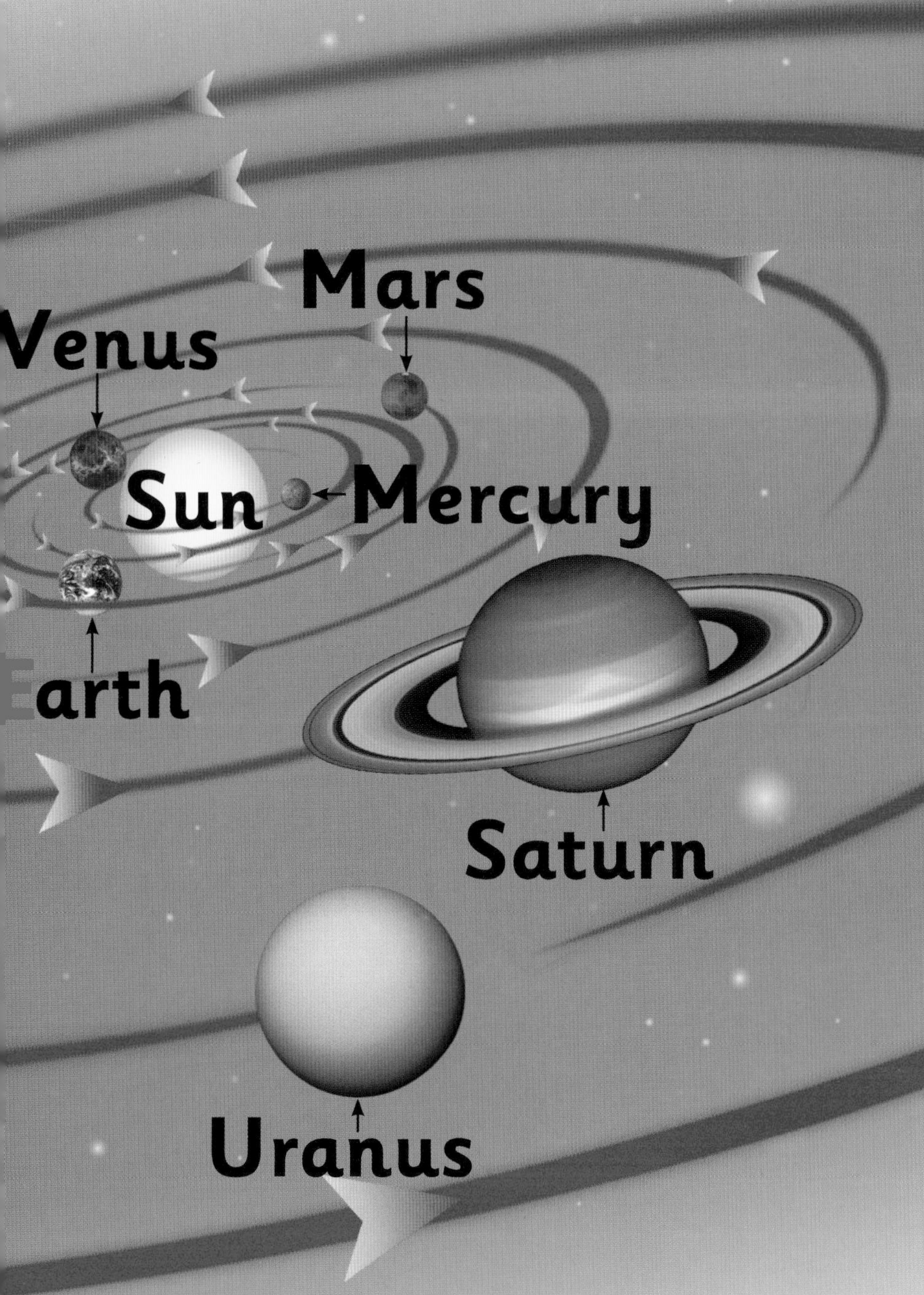

Can you see Earth (our world)?

Our world seems so small and space so big. Our world is very special: it is not too hot and not too cold, so people, animals and plants can live here!

The Earth, our Planet

I'm the right way up!
NORTH AMERICA
ATLANTIC OCEAN
1
2
3
4
AFRICA

Let's look at our world from space.

Can you see: **blue** sea and **green** land?
What shape is the world?
Now **can you draw** the whole world?

These children are looking at our globe.

This atlas will help you to find that our globe is really interesting.
The globe is for **ALL** of us!

Why don't we fall off our round world?

Answer: gravity keeps our feet on the ground!

Let's jump in a hot air balloon.

Pretend you are flying over our world. Let's take a closer look. Is it hot or cold, wet or dry, high or low?

ASIA
5
INDIAN OCEAN
I'm the right way up too!

Our world can be hot or cold, wet or dry, high or low.

Look at the balloons on the map. What would you need to pack when you visit these different places?

1 It is **cold** here.

2 It is **warm in summer** here and **cool in winter**.

3 It is **very hot and dry** here.

4 It is **hot and wet** here.

5 It is **high up** here.

Ideas for grown-ups

Imagine looking at the Earth from a spacecraft. You can see the whole world, like a round ball in space.

- ★ Talk about how it is shaped like a ball. Talk about the colours and what they mean.
- ★ Now you have had a good look, can the children draw the whole world like this? Just a rough sketch!
- ★ Imagine landing in different places and what you would need to wear.

Making Sense of Maps

Let's understand map colours.

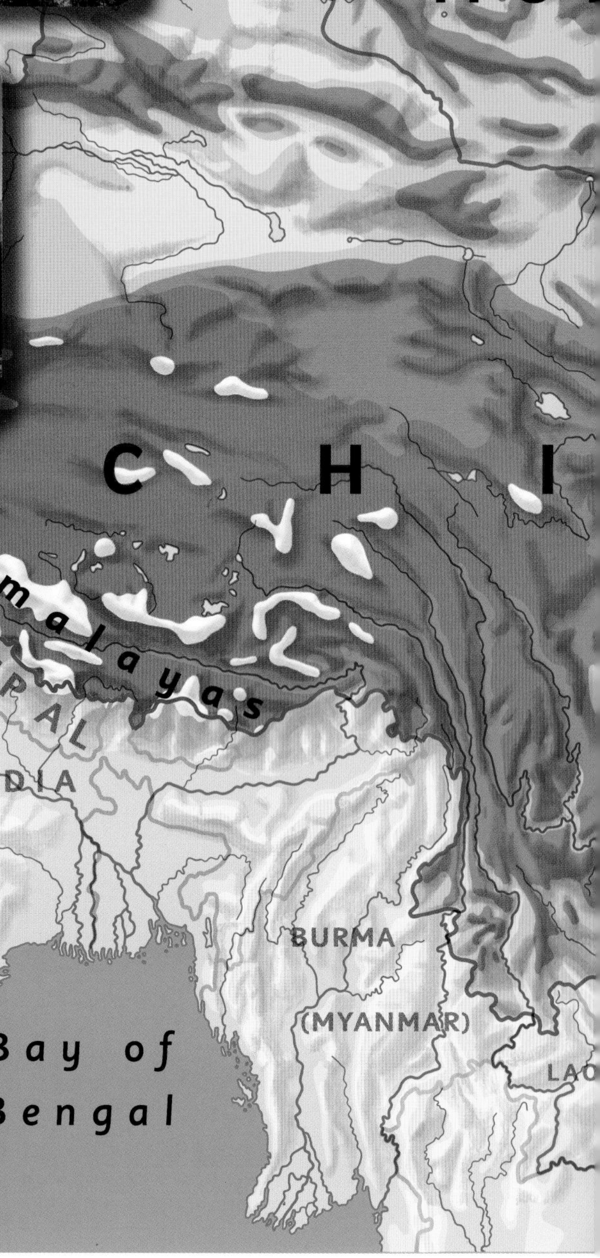

What is blue on the map?

Blue is for water – oceans, seas, lakes and rivers.

What is brown on the map?

Brown is for high land (mountains).

Can you spot yellow as well?

Yellow is for land 'in between' low land and high land.

What is green on the map?

Green is for low land.

What is red on the map?

Red lines show the edge of countries. Some cities are shown: look for ☆ or ●.

What is black on the map?

The **CAPITAL** letters are **COUNTRY** and **OCEAN** names. Other black writing tells us names of deserts, mountains, cities, and other exciting places!

Gobi Desert
Beijing
NORTH KOREA
SOUTH KOREA
JAPAN
TAIWAN
Hong Kong
PACIFIC OCEAN
PHILIPPINES

Can you understand scale?

Yes, you can!

A toy car is a 'scale model' of a real car. A real car is perhaps 50 or 100 times bigger. Even your doll or teddy bear are scale models!

Here's a rhyme to help you remember!

Water is **blue**,
Low land is **green**,
High land is **brown**,
Yellow's in between!

Find out about...

Sea and Land

There are 4 oceans on our planet.

Look for the big words on the blue sea.
There is much more sea than land on our planet.
The **PACIFIC OCEAN** is **SO** big!
It is bigger than **ALL** the world's land! Amazing!

There are nearly 200 countries in our world.

Each country has its own flag, money, stamps and capital city.

There are 7 continents on our planet.

Here are 6 of them – can you match them to the shapes on this map? Page 3 will help you. Find the extra continent on page 47! The biggest one has the smallest name: **ASIA**. Can you find it? Each continent has a colour, and we use these colours on all the map pages.

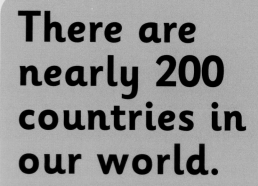

Can you find the **6 biggest countries**? Their 6 names and 6 flags are on the map. The photo shows flags outside the United Nations building in the USA.

These 5 countries have the most people.

1. **China** 1,314 million
2. **India** 1,095 million
3. **USA** 298 million
4. **Indonesia** 245 million
5. **Brazil** 188 million

ARCTIC OCEAN
RUSSIA
Russia
EUROPE
1
CHINA
Mediterranean Sea
ASIA
China
PACIFIC OCEAN
INDIA
AFRICA
2
4
INDIAN OCEAN
INDONESIA
ATLANTIC OCEAN
AUSTRALIA
Australia
ANTARCTICA
ANTARCTICA

Ideas for grown-ups

- ★ 'Big' and 'little' are concepts that young children cope with well – and they are very important concepts. Find the biggest ocean, continent, country!
- ★ Revisit this page after they have explored some other pages in this atlas ... then they can try to spot the 6 biggest countries.

Find out about...

The British Isles

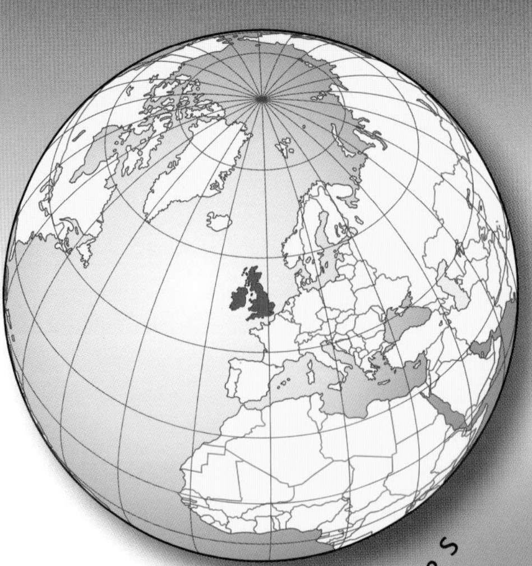

1 Let's go to London.

London is a capital city. Let's catch a **big red bus**! Can you see a big clock? It is called **Big Ben**.

3

Look for a dragon!

The flag of **Wales** has a red dragon on it. There aren't any real dragons in Wales!

2 Can you see the white horse?

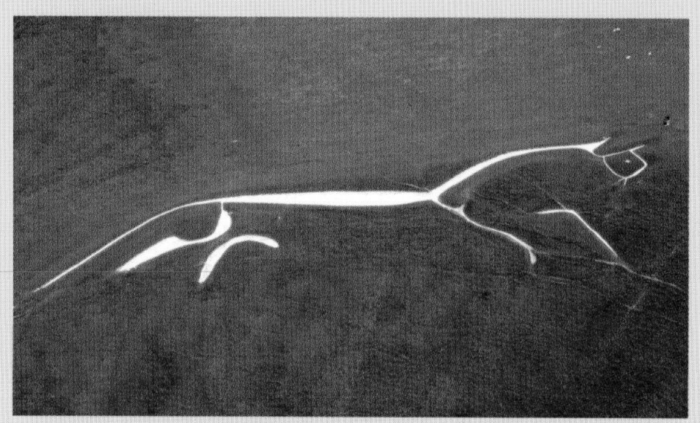

People have lived in Britain for thousands of years. Long ago people carved this giant picture into the hill. The hill is made of white chalk.

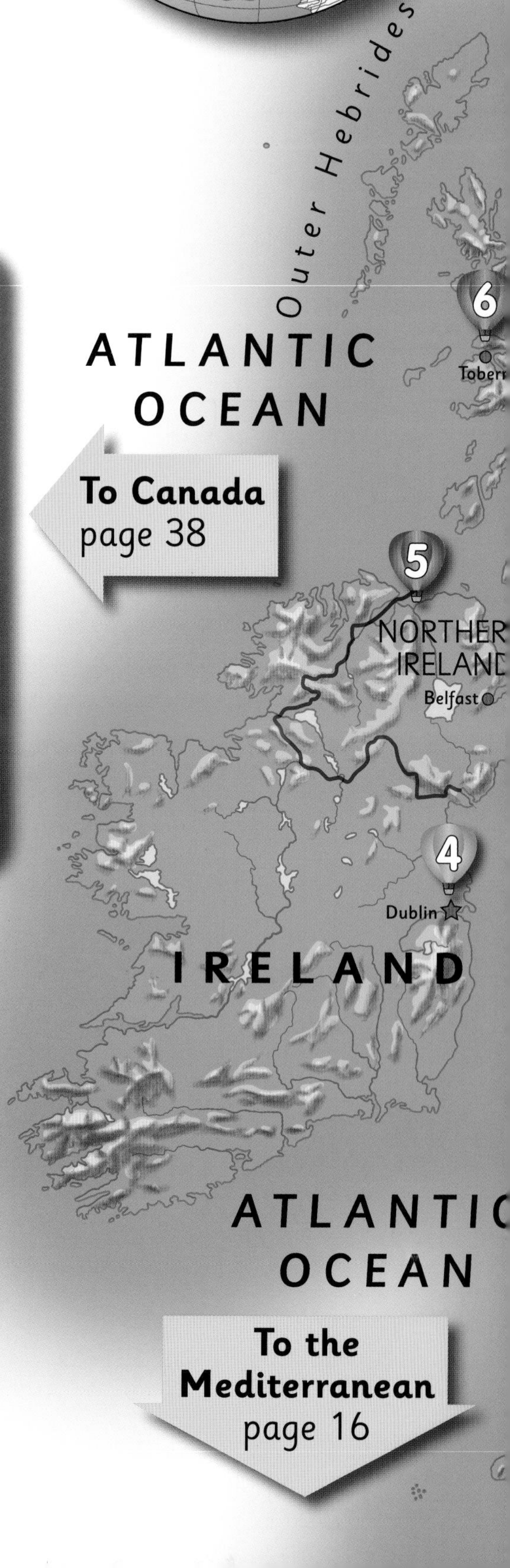

To Canada
page 38

To the Mediterranean
page 16

Shetland Islands
Orkney Islands
North Sea
SCOTLAND
Edinburgh
UNITED KINGDOM
Isle of Man
ish
ea
ENGLAND
WALES
Cardiff
London
Isle of Wight
0 50 km 100 km 200 km 300 km
English Channel
FRANCE

To the North Pole page 46

To Western Europe page 14

4 Let's see dancing and hear music.

St Patrick's Day is a special day in **Ireland** and for Irish people all over the world. What colours are the people wearing?

5 Let's jump on stepping stones.

These amazing stones are called the **Giant's Causeway**. Most are 6-sided shapes. They were made long ago by lava from a volcano.

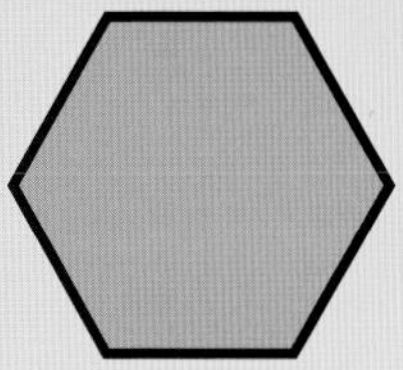

6 Let's get on a boat.

Can you see all the different coloured houses? **Scotland** has lots of islands. This is Tobermory on the island of Mull. Can you see more islands on the map?

Ideas for grown-ups

- Talk about London, the capital of England. This is where the Queen lives and Parliament is. What do the children know about London?
- Can you find other hexagons (6-sided shapes) like the stones of the Giant's Causeway? Look at nuts and bolts, or a honeycomb.
- Look at the map. Which is biggest: England or Wales or Scotland? Which is smallest?

Find out about...

Western Europe

1 Lots of trees grow in Sweden.

The wood can be used to make houses, paper and wooden train sets!

2 Let's play with Lego.

Here is a model of a village at Legoland in **Denmark**. Lego was invented in Denmark.

To the North Pole page 46

To Canada page 38

Ideas for grown-ups

- Look on the map for the low land of Holland (the Netherlands) and the high land of Switzerland and Austria.
- Can you find two countries with no seaside?
- Can you find an ice sheet on Iceland?
- The two smallest countries both begin with L – can you find them?

3 A snowy owl

is white, so it is hard to see in snow!

NORWAY
SWEDEN
FINLAND
RUSSIA
Baltic Sea
ea
DENMARK
ETHERLANDS
GERMANY
POLAND
ELGIUM
UXEMBOURG
CZECH REPUBLIC
AUSTRIA
C E
LIECHTENSTEIN
SWITZERLAND
SLOVENIA
CROATIA
ITALY
0
500 km
1,000 km

To Russia page 20

To Africa page 30

4 Look at the windmills.

They are not really windmills. They are **wind turbines**. They use wind to make electricity.

5 The flag of France is called the Tricolor.

Tricolor means **3 colours** in French. What are the 3 colours of the French flag? Can you draw a tricolor?

6 Can you...

make a **Christingle**? It was invented in Germany to teach children the meaning of Christmas. It is an orange (represents the world), a candle in the top (for Jesus), and 4 little sticks with sweets on (= the fruits of the world and the 4 seasons).

Find out about...

Mediterranean Europe

1

Can you see people dancing?

These people are flamenco dancers, in **Spain**. The music is called flamenco too.

3 Let's play on the beach.

The countries around the Mediterranean Sea have hot dry summers, so people love to come here on holiday. Can you see ... a hotel? ... palm trees? ... people swimming?

2 I am a lynx.

A lynx is a small wild cat. This lynx is very rare now but some can still be found in the mountains of Spain and Portugal.

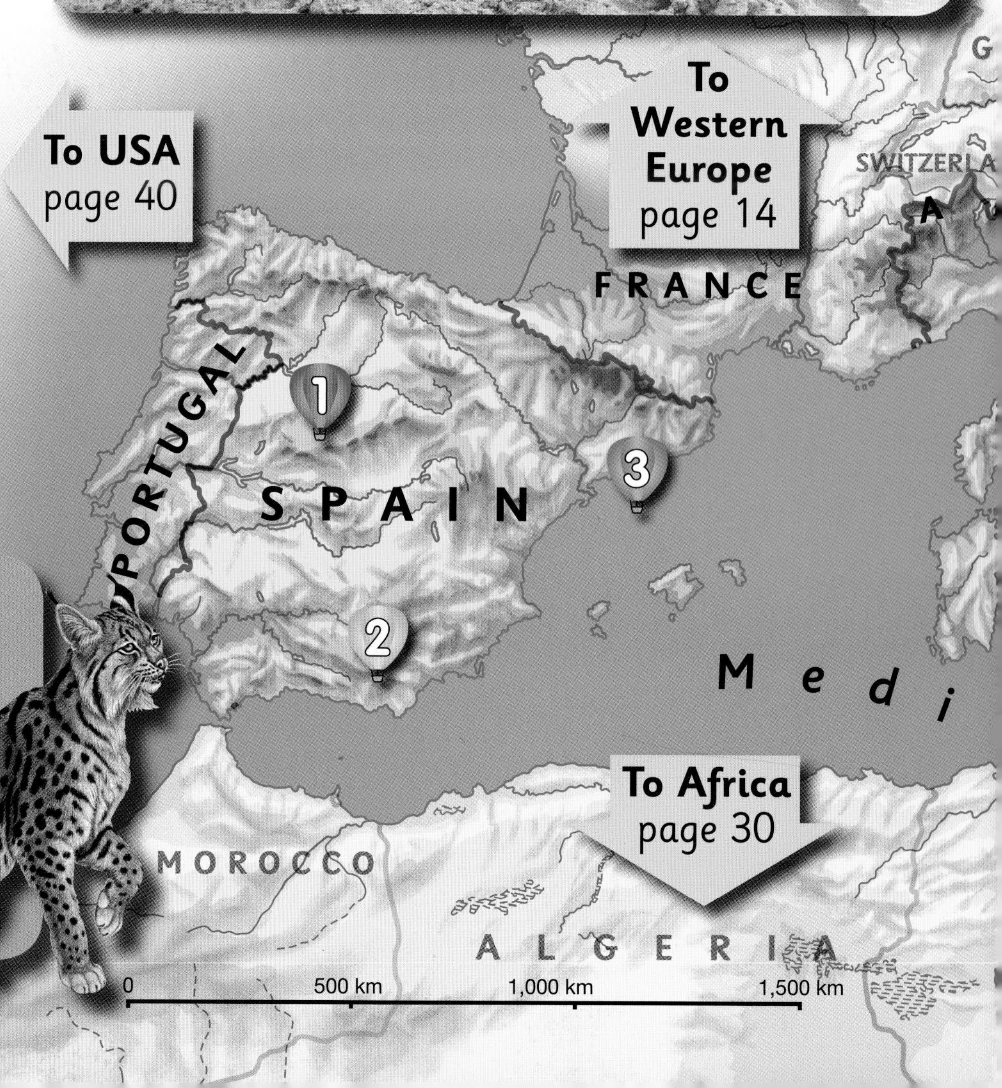

To USA page 40

To Western Europe page 14

To Africa page 30

4 Will this tower fall over?

It is the leaning tower of Pisa in **Italy**. It is 800 years old. Now concrete has been put below it to make sure it is safe. The tower is next to the cathedral.

5 Can you run fast?

The ladies in the picture are the fastest runners from their countries. The **Olympic Games** were invented in Greece 2,000 years ago. And in 2004 they were held in Greece again. Can you see the Olympic sign on the ladies' vests?

Ideas for grown-ups

★ Can you **taste** the Mediterranean? Look for tomatoes, oranges, olives, grapes – don't forget some sardines! Pasta from Italy, paella from Spain, hummus from Greece! Have a Mediterranean feast!

★ Can you draw the Olympic symbol?

ANY
AUSTRIA
SLOVENIA
CROATIA
BOSNIA
SERBIA
ROMANIA
MONTENEGRO
KOSOVO
BULGARIA
MACEDONIA
ALBANIA
GREECE
ITALY
5
6
rranean Sea

To Eastern Europe page 18

To Asia page 24

6 What is growing on the trees?

Oranges and lemons grow well around the Mediterranean. They like warm wet winters and hot dry summers. Can you see mountains too?

Find out about...

Eastern Europe

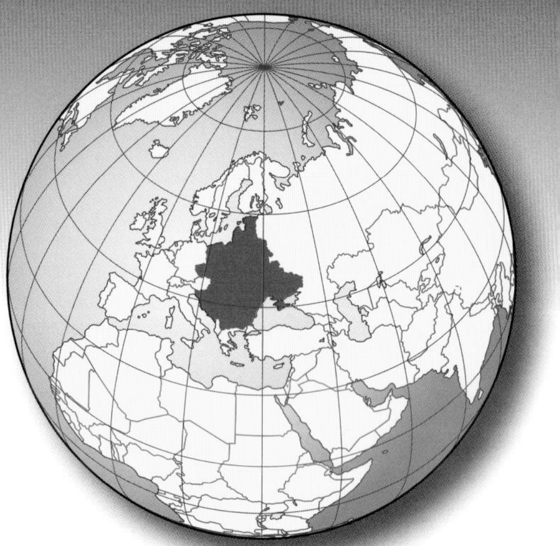

1 Let's visit a factory.

There are some big factories in **Poland**.
This factory is making iron.

2 Can you see 2 flags?

These flags belong to 2 countries: the **Czech Republic** and the **Slovak Republic**. Before 1990 there was only 1 country called Czechoslovakia!

3 There are big mountains here.

The mountains are called the **Carpathians**. There are pine forests and ski slopes.

SWEDEN
Baltic Sea
ESTONIA
LATVIA
LITHUANIA
[PART OF RUSSIA]
GERMANY
POLAND
BEL
CZECH REPUBLIC
SLOVAK REPUBLIC
U K
Carpathian Mountains
AUSTRIA
HUNGARY
MO
SLOVENIA
CROATIA
ROMANIA
BOSNIA
SERBIA
MONTENEGRO
KOSOVO
BULGARIA
MACEDONIA
ITALY
GREECE
1
2
3
4
5
6

To the North Pole page 46

To Africa page 30

Ideas for grown-ups

- ★ This area has changed a lot since you were a child! If you have an old atlas you could try playing a 'spot the difference' game with the children! Look for some new countries like Ukraine and Moldova.
- ★ Can you spot some countries with NO seaside?
- ★ Try tasting some Eastern European food, e.g. goulash from Hungary.

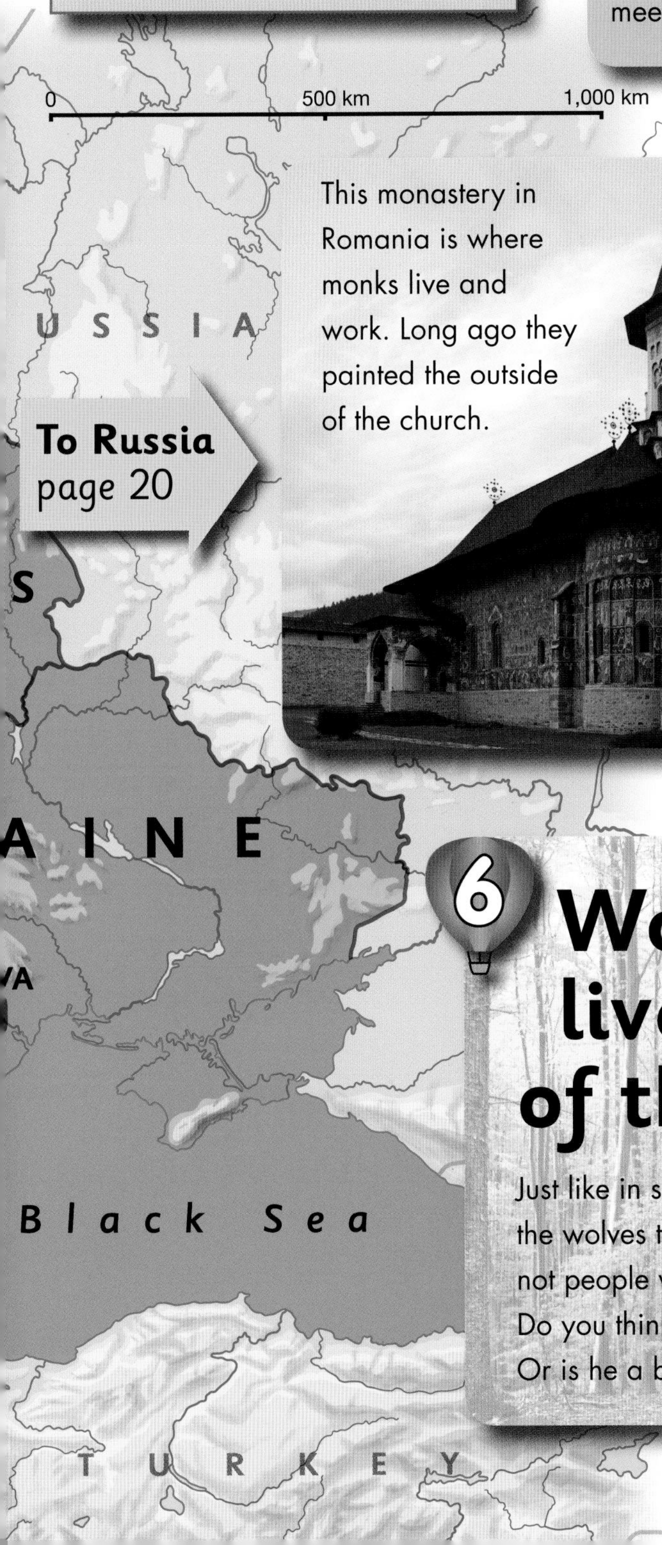

To Russia
page 20

4 Can you guess what this is?

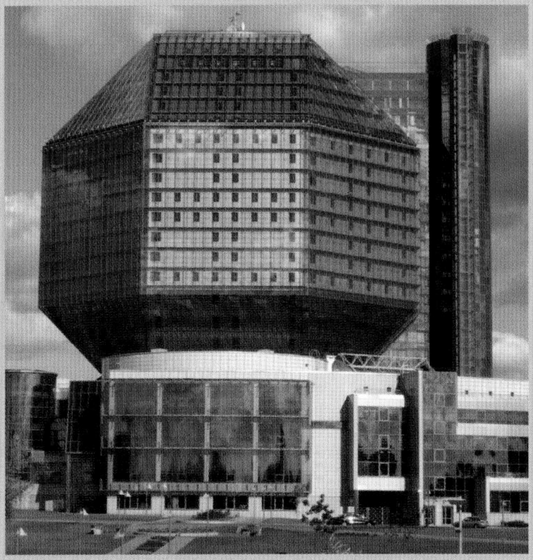

This amazing building in Belarus is a **library**! At night it is covered in lights that change colour.
Can you count how many countries meet **Belarus**? 3 or **5** or 7?

5 Let's visit Romania!

This monastery in Romania is where monks live and work. Long ago they painted the outside of the church.

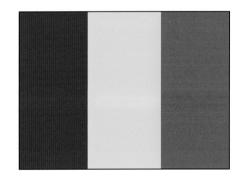

This is the flag of **Romania**.

6 Wolves still live in some of the forests.

Just like in some fairy tales! But now it is the wolves that need protecting from people, not people who need protecting from wolves.
Do you think this is a big, bad wolf?
Or is he a big, good, strong wolf?

Find out about...

Russia and its Neighbours

1 The Amur tiger is the biggest tiger.

It lives in **Russia**. There are not many tigers left, so all of them need looking after.

2 A space-man from Russia.

Russia sent the first person into space in 1963. The astronaut in this stamp looks very happy.

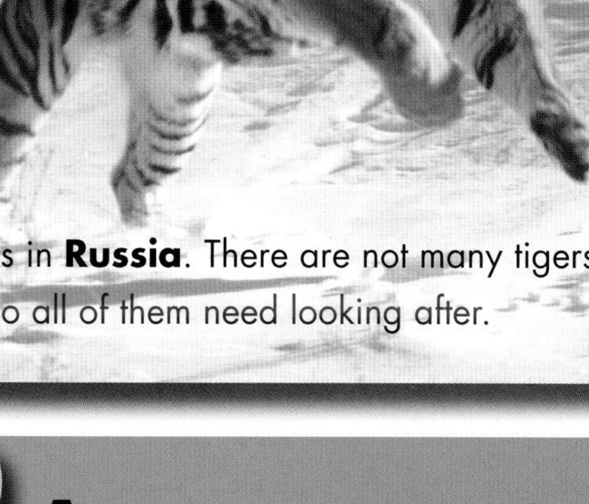

3 We live in a flat.

Can you see the block of flats where we live? Many people in Russia live in flats. Winters in Russia are **very cold** so we wear warm clothes. The snow is fun!

NORWAY
SWEDEN
FINLAND
ESTONIA
LATVIA
LITHUANIA
BELARUS
3
Moscow
2
Ural Mountains
RUS
5
KAZAKHSTAN
Black Sea
Caspian Sea
GEORGIA
TURKEY
ARMENIA
AZERBAIJAN
UZBEKISTAN
6
TURKMENISTAN
KYRGYZSTAN
TAJIKISTAN
SYRIA
IRAQ
IRAN
AFGHANISTAN

To Eastern Europe page 18

I can see 2 trains.

This is the **world's longest railway**! It takes 7 days and nights for these trains to cross Russia on the Trans-Siberian Railway. The trains travel past millions of trees!

What am I?

I am a **porcupine** from **Kazakhstan**. I am prickly like a hedgehog. But my spikes are even longer. My spikes are good for scaring other animals away. I dig borrows in the ground to live in. I can grow to nearly a metre long.

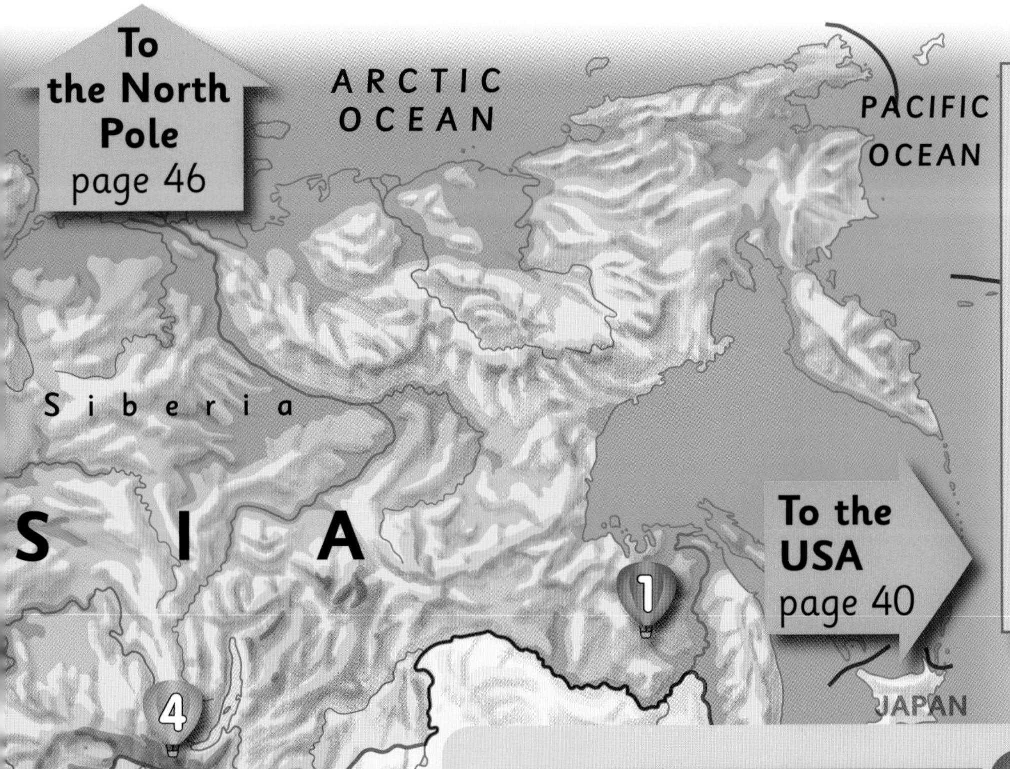

To the North Pole page 46

To the USA page 40

To India and Southern Asia page 24

Ideas for grown-ups

Spin the globe – see how Russia is SO MUCH bigger than any other country. East to west, it stretches further than any CONTINENT! Young children love opposites. On this map we can find:

- ★ Very cold lands – and very hot lands.
- ★ Very high lands and very low lands – the Caspian Sea is below sea level.
- ★ Very wet and very dry lands.
- ★ The names of the countries south of Russia are as long and exciting as dinosaur names!

I can see the Moon.

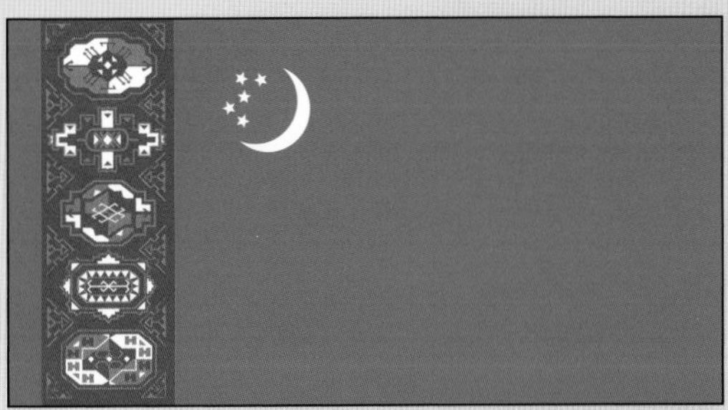

This is the flag of **Turkmenistan**. What can you see on this flag?

Find out about...

The Middle East

1 Let's eat a date.

Dates grow in desert lands with dry air. Can you see how the dates and the palm fronds grow from the top of the **palm tree**?

2 Let's look for oil.

Oil has made some people rich. But oil pollutes and it will run out one day.

EUROPE
To Russia page 20
Black Sea
ARMENIA
TURKEY
Mediterranean Sea
CYPRUS
3
SYRIA
LEBANON
ISRAEL
IRAQ
4
JORDAN
KU
EGYPT
2
This way to North Africa page 30
Red Sea
5
Mecca
SAUD
AFRICA
SUDAN
This way to Southern Africa page 32
ETHIOPIA

Let's find a tree.

It is not dry everywhere. This cedar tree is so green and special that it is on the flag of **Lebanon**.

Let's visit Israel.

Most people in Israel are Jews. This family is celebrating Passover with special food. On Saturday (Sabbath) many people go to the Synagogue to worship God.

Let's go to Mecca.

Mecca is a very important city for Muslims. The Hajj is when Muslims all over the world come to Mecca. Can you see all the people praying? Almost everyone is wearing white.

This way to India page 24

Ideas for grown-ups

- Can you taste and feel a date? Is it sticky? Is it sweet? Look at the date palm picture to talk about how they grow, and how they might be picked!
- Talk about oil, how important it is for lots of things we use every day. Talk about the problems too.
- Talk about Judaism, Islam and Christianity; see if you can find out more about Jewish, Muslim and Christian festivals and customs.

Find out about...

India and Southern Asia

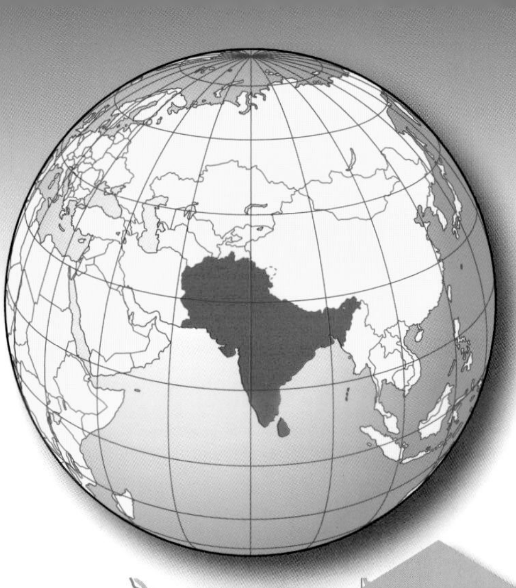

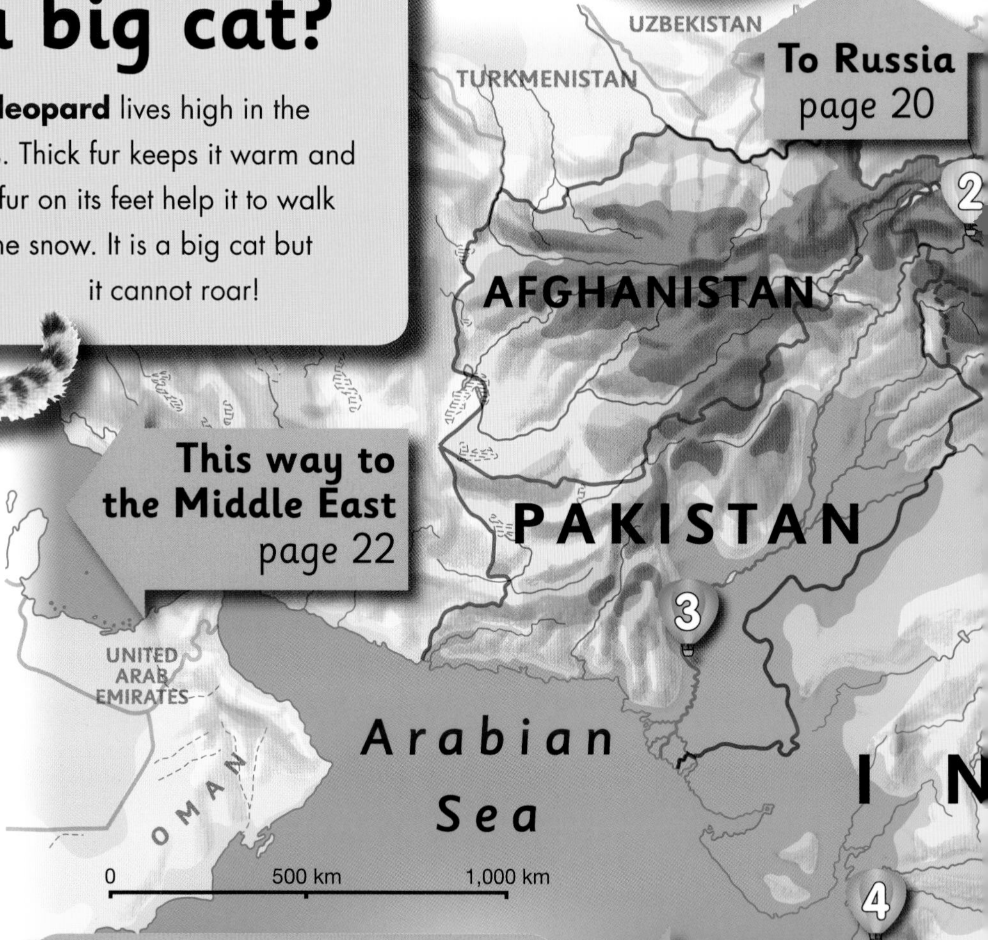
UZBEKISTAN
TURKMENISTAN
AFGHANISTAN
PAKISTAN
UNITED ARAB EMIRATES
OMAN
Arabian Sea
IN
0
500 km
1,000 km

To Russia page 20

This way to the Middle East page 22

This way to Africa page 30

1 Can you see a big cat?

This **snow leopard** lives high in the mountains. Thick fur keeps it warm and the fur on its feet help it to walk in the snow. It is a big cat but it cannot roar!

2 I can see a mountain.

The **Himalayas** have all of the 10 highest mountains in the world. This is K2 – it is nearly as high as Mount Everest.

3 Learning to read.

This stamp shows children and grown-ups in Pakistan learning to read.

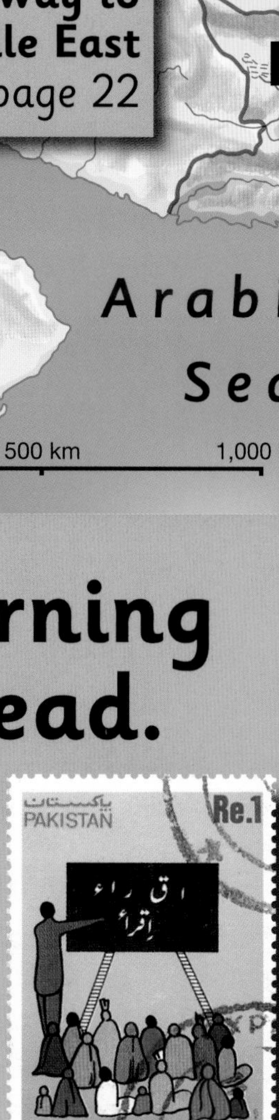

INDIAN OCEAN

This way to Antarctica page 47

Let's find a Tuk-tuk.

Tuk-tuks are Indian taxis with 3 wheels. There is no door, so be careful not to fall out! You can hear all the noise of an Indian city!

Let's light a lamp.

Divali is celebrated by Hindus and Sikhs. Lots of lamps are lit, there is special food, and families like to be together.

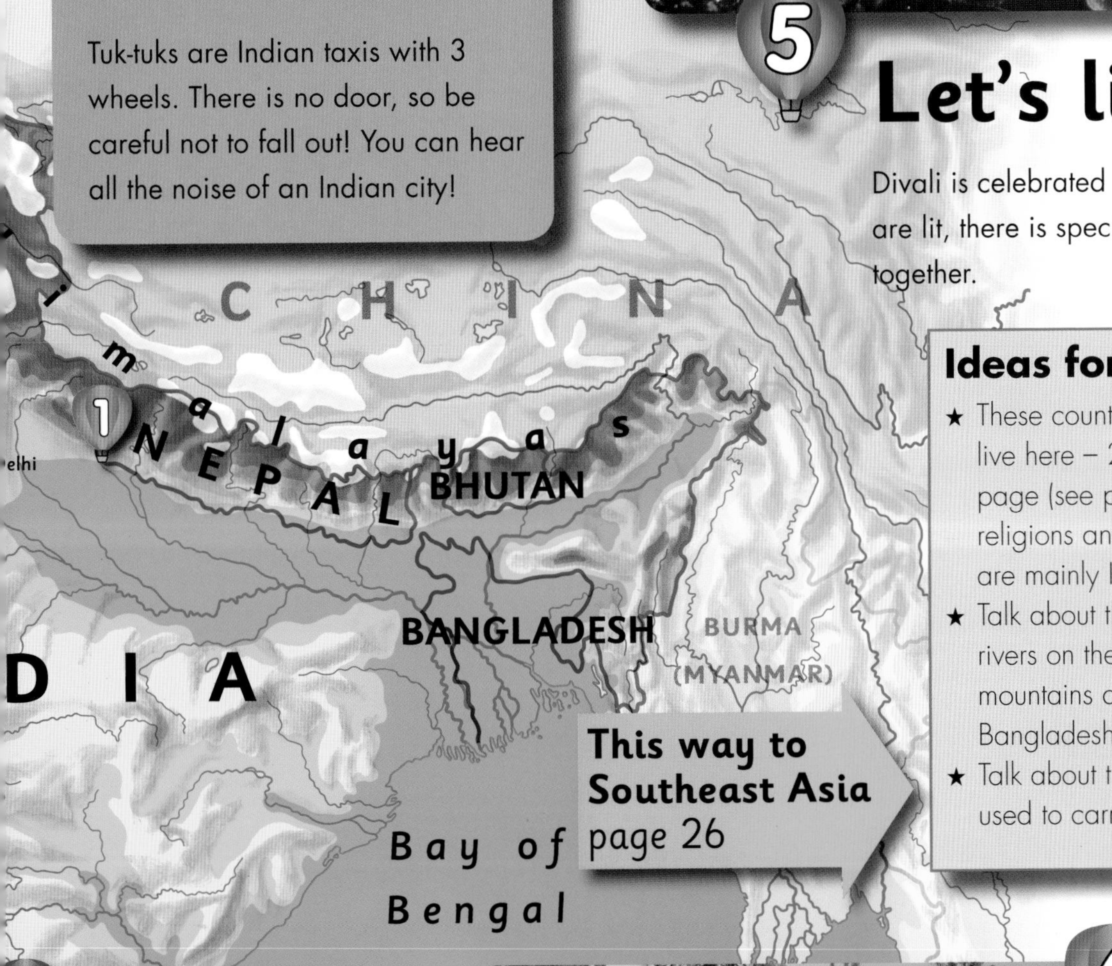

This way to Southeast Asia page 26

Ideas for grown-ups

- ★ These countries are very important. Lots of people live here – 2 of the 'top 5' countries are on this page (see page 11). There are many different religions and traditions. Pakistan and Bangladesh are mainly Islamic countries.
- ★ Talk about the high mountains and look at the rivers on the map: they bring the water from the mountains all year. Talk about the low delta of Bangladesh which easily floods.
- ★ Talk about the elephants. Some elephants are used to carry logs and work very hard.

Let's help look after elephants.

People look after these elephants that have no mum or dad. Every day they take them to the river for a bath.

Find out about...
Southeast Asia

1 A tractor works on fields.

The caterpillar tracks help the tractor on the wet fields. Can you see the plough behind the tractor? And the factories, far away? This stamp comes from **Laos**.

2 Let's get wet!

The festival of Songkran in **Thailand** is fun! Lots of people and elephants throw water! It is a Buddhist festival for New Year (in April).

3 Let's visit a lost city.

No-one lives in Angkor Wat now. Can you see the reflections of these very old temples?

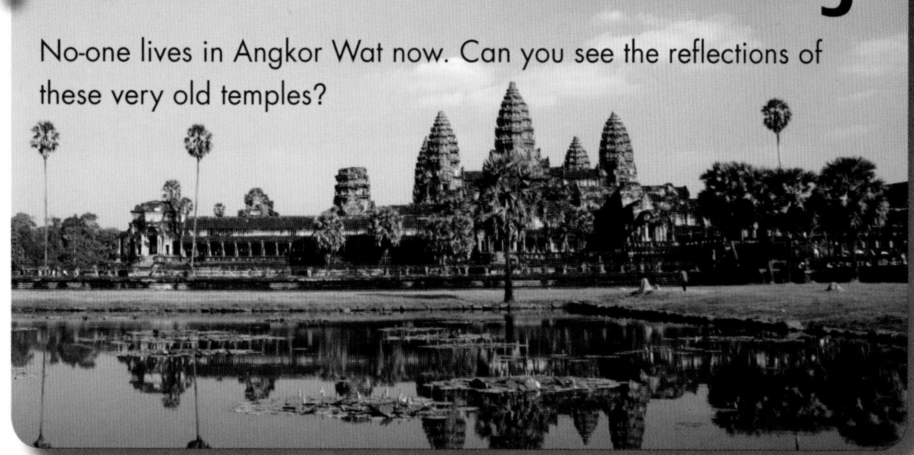

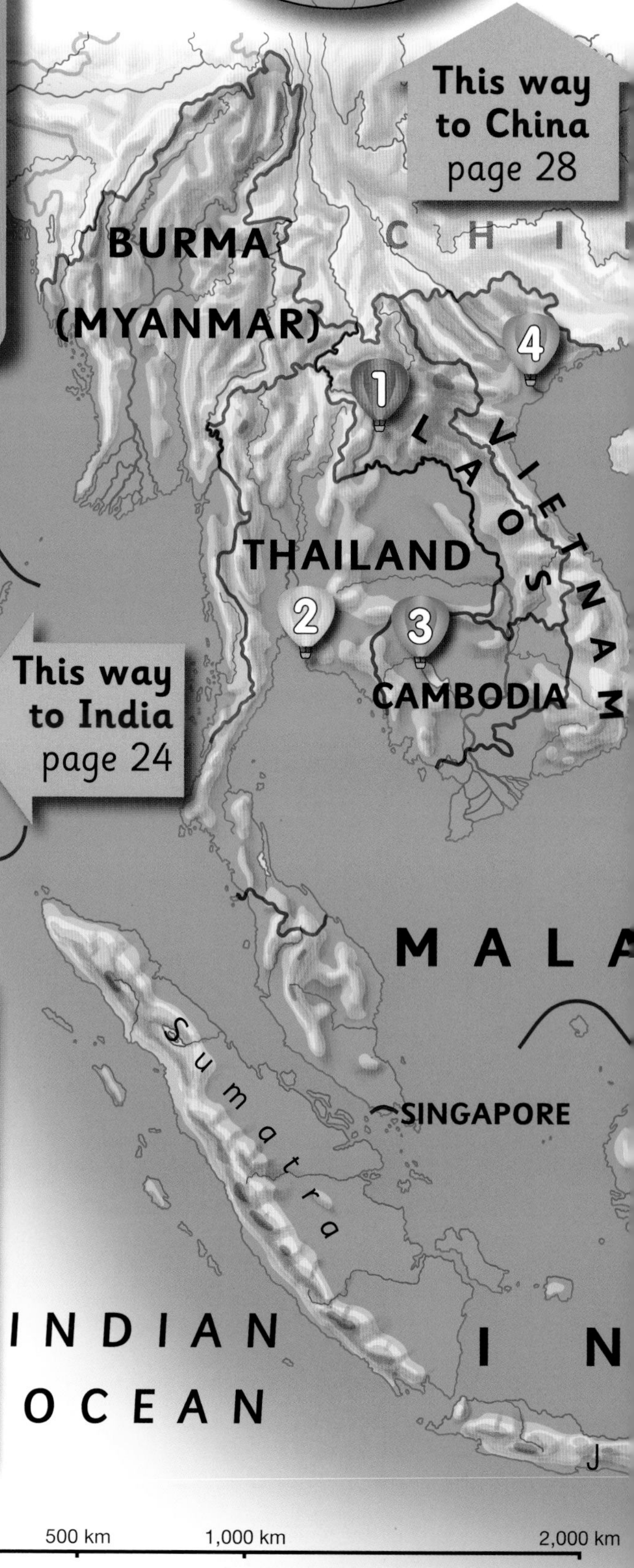
BURMA
(MYANMAR)
CHI
THAILAND
LAOS
VIETNAM
CAMBODIA
MALA
SINGAPORE
Sumatra
INDIAN
OCEAN
I N
1
2
3
4
0
500 km
1,000 km
2,000 km

This way to China page 28

This way to India page 24

4 A traffic jam in Vietnam.

Can you see lots of people on bikes and motorbikes?

5 Orang-utans live in the forests of Borneo.

They are rare and amazing. Tourists come to see them, but some of the forests are being cut down. Borneo is a big island: **Indonesia** is a country with lots of islands and lots of people.

6 Beware of volcanoes!

There are more volcanoes in Southeast Asia than anywhere else on Earth. Can you see people in the boat escaping to safety? Can you see which country issued this stamp?

PILIPINAS
70s
PANGHIMPAPAWID
TAAL VOLCANO
ERUPTION-1965

A
PACIFIC OCEAN
South China Sea
6
PHILIPPINES
SIA
BRUNEI
5
Borneo
DONESIA
EAST TIMOR
a
AUSTRALIA

To Australia page 36

Ideas for grown-ups

- ★ Have a go at eating rice with chopsticks. If the rice is sticky, it is easier!
- ★ Buddhism and Islam are important religions in the countries on this map.
- ★ Indonesia has the world's 4th largest population.
- ★ Farming, forests, people and rare animals are the important themes here.

Find out about...

East Asia

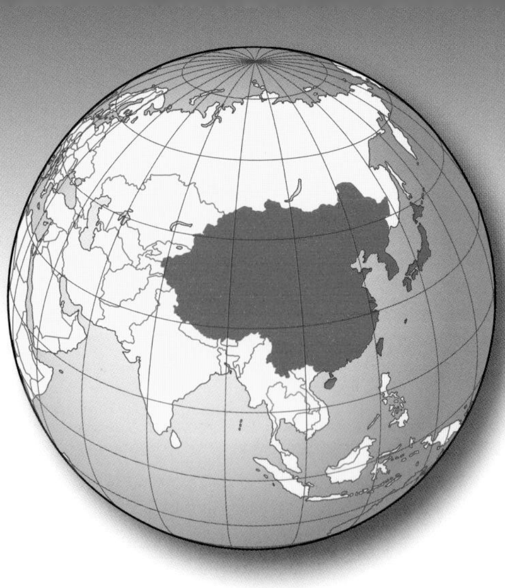

1 The flag of Mongolia.

Mongolia is a big country with **NO** seaside and very cold winters.

To Russia
page 20

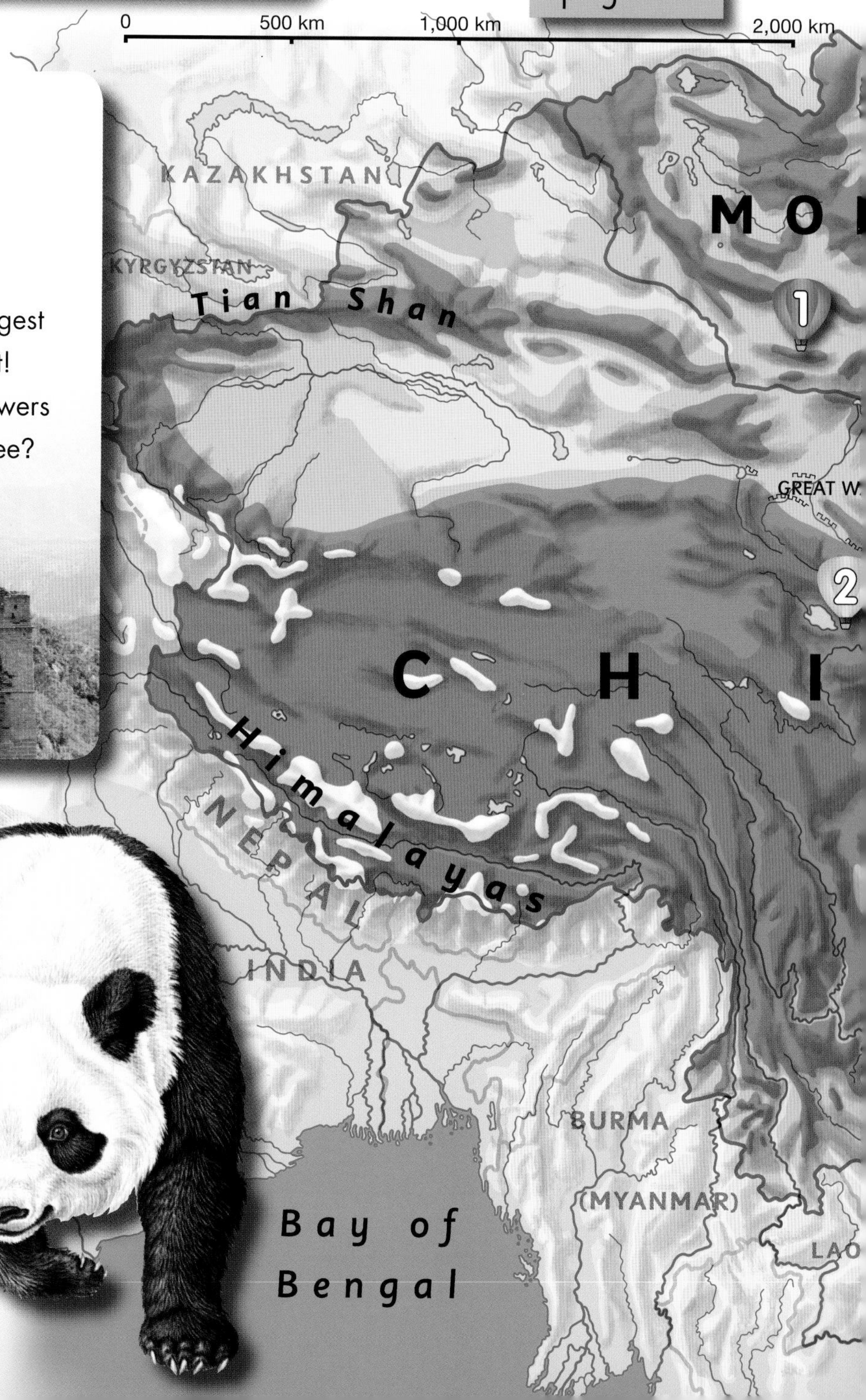
0
500 km
1,000 km
2,000 km
KAZAKHSTAN
KYRGYZSTAN
Tian Shan
MO
1
GREAT W
2
C H I
Himalayas
NEPAL
INDIA
BURMA
(MYANMAR)
Bay of Bengal
LAO

2 Let's see the Great Wall.

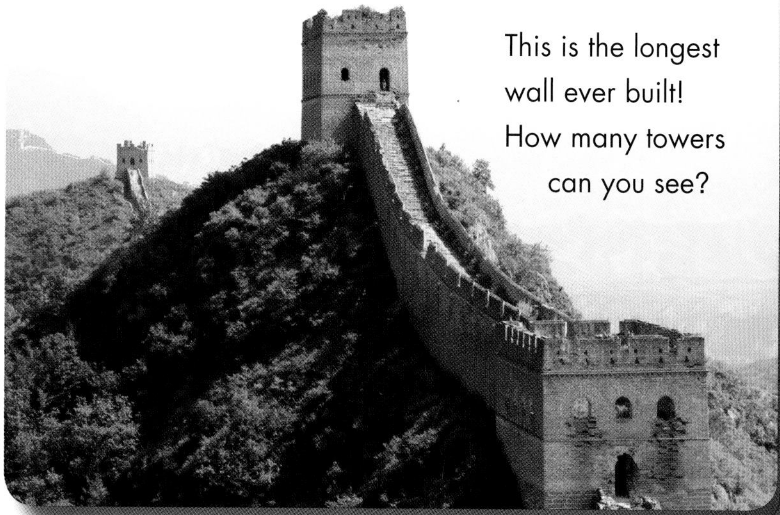

This is the longest wall ever built! How many towers can you see?

3 Let's find a Panda.

Pandas only live in China, in a few of the mountains. They are rare. They eat **bamboo** all day!

4 Let's find a friend.

Most children in China have no brothers and no sisters, so friends are important! More people live in China than in any other country.

5 I can see a dragon.

It is a giant puppet. People make it dance for **Chinese New Year** in Hong Kong.

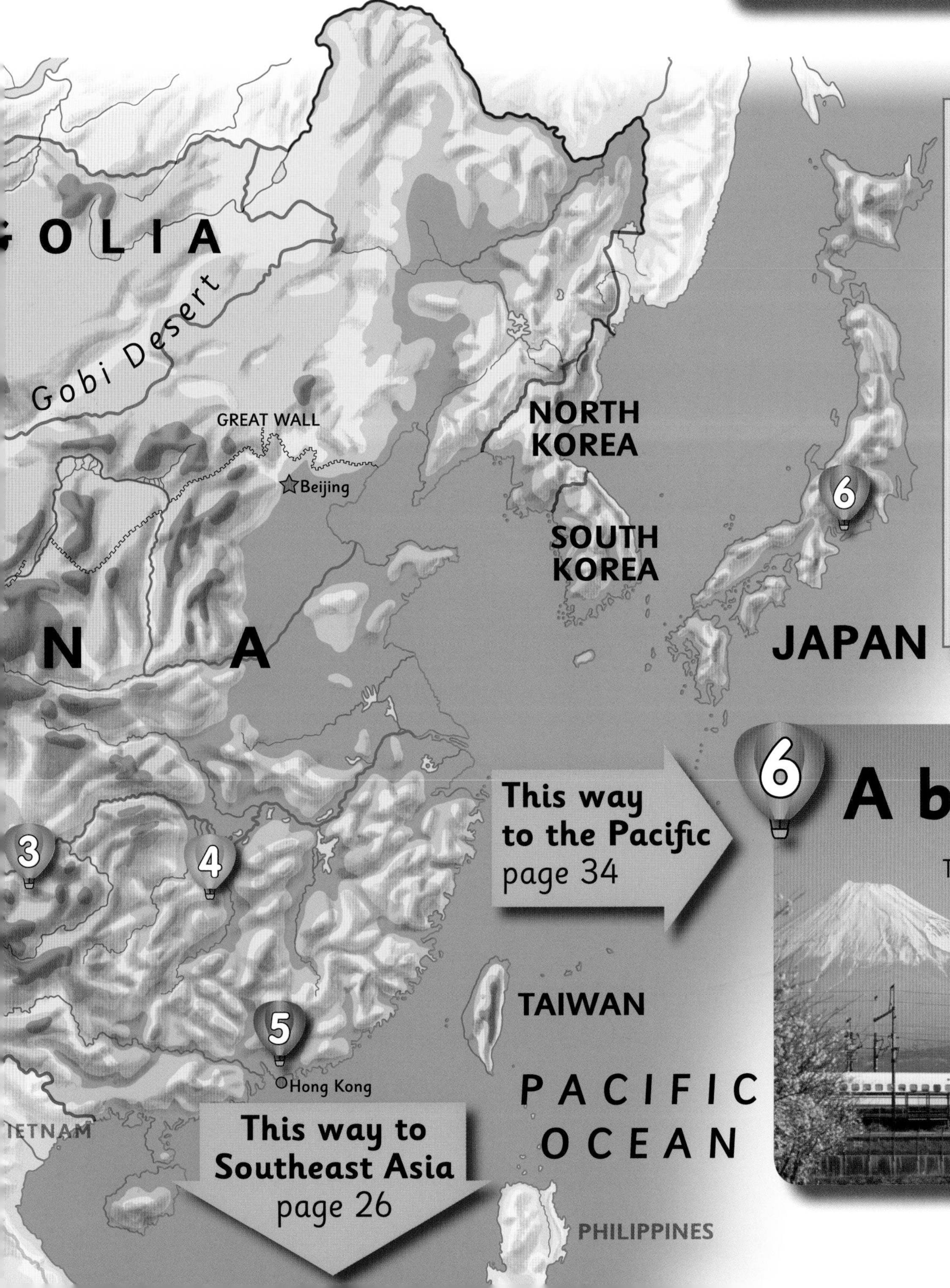

GOLIA
Gobi Desert
GREAT WALL
Beijing
NORTH KOREA
SOUTH KOREA
JAPAN
N A
3
4
5
6
Hong Kong
TAIWAN
PACIFIC OCEAN
IETNAM
PHILIPPINES

Ideas for grown-ups

- ★ Talk about China's one-child policy. It has run for more than a generation, so many children have no aunties or uncles or cousins, as well as no brothers or sisters.
- ★ Look for toys from China: look underneath for the 'Made in...' label. Can you make a rubbing? Look for Korea as well as China.
- ★ Talk about the Great Wall – it is over 6,000 km long!
- ★ Every Chinese year has an animal. See if you can find out the birth year and animal of the children.

This way to the Pacific page 34

6 A bullet train.

This train is very fast, but not really as fast as a bullet! Can you see Mount Fuji? It is an old **volcano**.

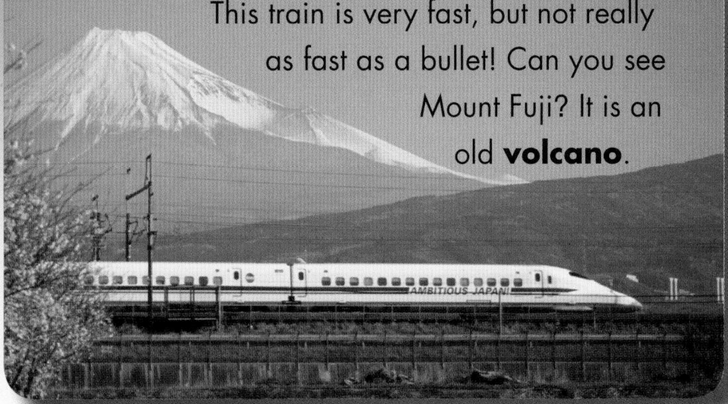

This way to Southeast Asia page 26

Find out about...

Northern Africa

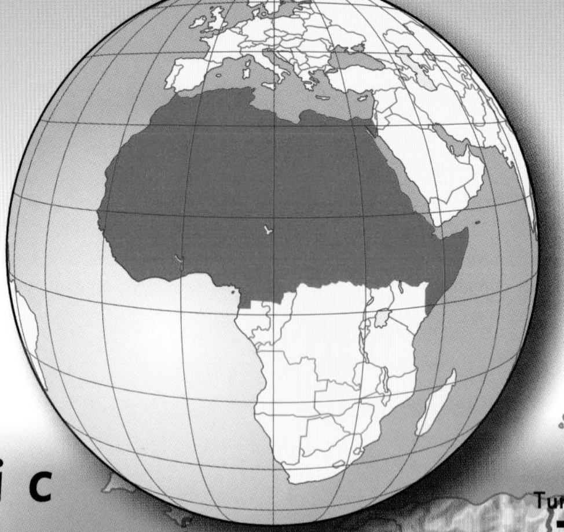

Atlantic Ocean
MOROCCO
Tunis
TUNISIA
ALGERIA
WESTERN SAHARA
Sahara
MAURITANIA
MALI
NIGE
SENEGAL
GAMBIA
GUINEA-BISSAU
GUINEA
SIERRA LEONE
LIBERIA
IVORY COAST
BURKINA FASO
GHANA
TOGO
BENIN
NIGERIA
CAMEROO
EQUATORIAL GUINEA
SAO TOME AND PRINCIPE
GABO
5
4

1 Pyramids in Egypt.

The Pyramids of Egypt are **so big**! They were built 4,500 years ago. There were no diggers or dump trucks to help the people.

2 Crocodile in the swamp!

Crocodiles can be found in Africa and grow to 5 metres long. Be careful not to get near them – they are very dangerous!

To Central America page 42

3 See a hyena.

Hyenas eat meat. Their call sounds like laughing.

A busy market in Nigeria.

4

Here is a big city in Nigeria. Millions of people live in this country. Can you see what is for sale? Tomatoes? Mats?

0 500 km 1,000 km 2,000 km
SYRIA
Mediterranean Sea
IRAQ
JORDAN
EGYPT
IBYA
SAUDI ARABIA
Red Sea
esert
CHAD
SUDAN
ERITREA
YEMEN
DJIBOUTI
ETHIOPIA
SOMALI REPUBLIC
CENTRAL AFRICAN REPUBLIC
CONGO
UGANDA
KENYA
Indian Ocean
1
2

To Europe page 16

To Asia page 24

To Central Africa page 32

5 Let's go to Togo!

This flag is the flag of Togo.
It has **green** for farming,
and **gold** – for gold!
And a **white** star for peace.

6 Let's visit Tunis!

This is a mosque in Tunis, the capital city. Can you guess which country it is in? Its name is a clue!

Ideas for grown-ups

On this map, there's a HUGE desert – yet there's FOREST in West Africa!

- ★ Make a desert in a sand tray! Make some sand dunes, add a camel, or a 4-wheel drive vehicle. Make palm trees by cutting slits into green paper. Wrap the cut paper round a brown tube or stick. Spread out the palm fronds! Make a tent for nomads or tourists – use brown paper.
- ★ Remember African camels have only 1 hump – not 2.
- ★ Encourage imagination: talk about how hot and dusty the desert is.
  – Remember to wear a hat and have lots of water!
  – If there is a sand storm, cover your face!

Find out about...

Central and Southern Africa

1 Let's look at a canoe.

It was dug out of a great big tree trunk. Big trees grow in the rainforest of **Congo**.

Gorillas in Congo.

There are not many gorillas left. If the forest is cut down, gorillas lose their home.

To the rest of Africa page 30

CAMEROON
Congo
GABON
CONGO
DEMOCRATIC REPUBLIC OF THE CONGO
CABINDA
ANGOLA
Z
4
NAMIBIA
BOTSWAN
5
SOUT
AFRIC
ATLANTIC OCEAN

To South America page 44

2 Can you see big animals?

These **zebras** and **giraffes** are in a national park in Kenya. Did you know zebras and giraffes only live in Africa?

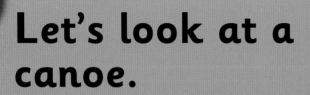

Ideas for grown-ups

Plan an exciting expedition to Africa. Will you...

★ Take a balloon-safari over a game park? [Beware of thunderstorms!]
★ Travel along the River Congo in a dug-out canoe? [Beware of rapids!]
★ Fly over the Victoria Falls in a microlight?
★ Travel overland from Kenya to South Africa by bus and train?
★ Swim in a tropical ocean? [Beware of sharks!]

A happy baby.

PREVENTIVE MEDICINE
NUTRITION
POSTAGE
Clinics
ZAMBIA 15n

This baby is happy and healthy. He is being weighed at a clinic. Some babies and children are not so happy or healthy, where there is war or when there isn't enough food.

The Victoria Falls are fantastic!

These **waterfalls** are on the River Zambezi, between Zambia and Zimbabwe. Remember the 3 Zs!

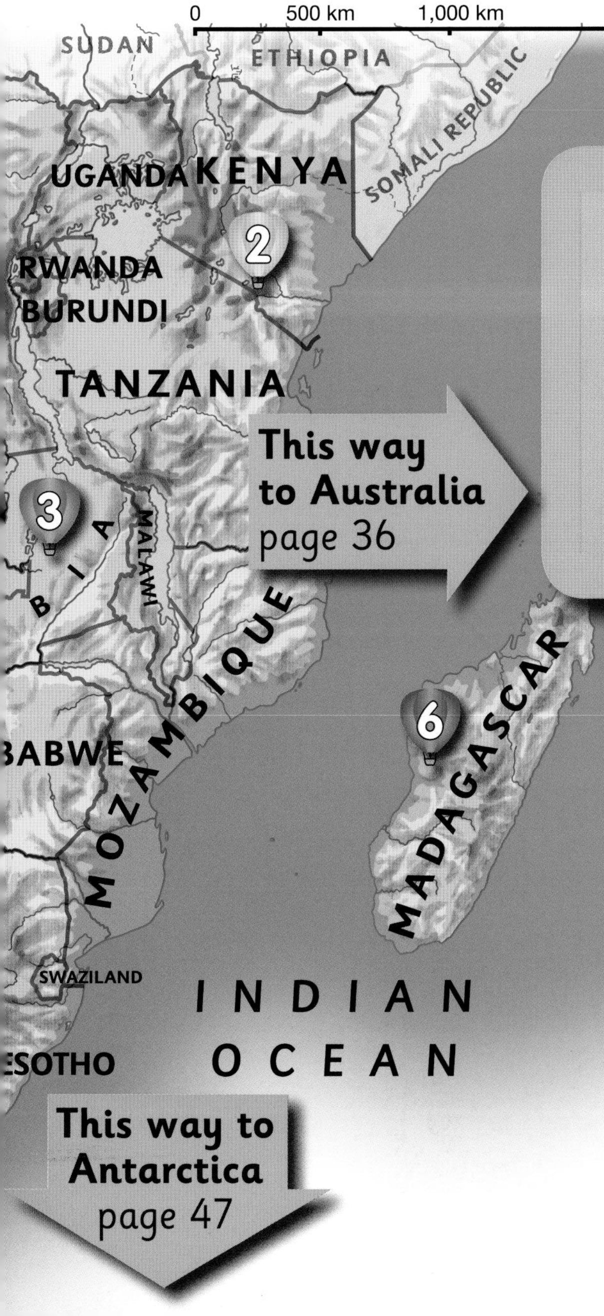
0
500 km
1,000 km
2,000 km
SUDAN
ETHIOPIA
SOMALI REPUBLIC
UGANDA
KENYA
2
RWANDA
BURUNDI
TANZANIA
3
MALAWI
MOZAMBIQUE
6
MADAGASCAR
SWAZILAND
INDIAN
OCEAN

This way to Australia page 36

This way to Antarctica page 47

Diamonds are so tiny.

But the great hole at Kimberley in South Africa is **SO** big ... because people worked so hard to dig out the tiny diamonds!

Look at that stripy tail!

It belongs to a lemur. Lemurs live on **Madagascar**, a big island east of Africa.

Find out about...
The Pacific

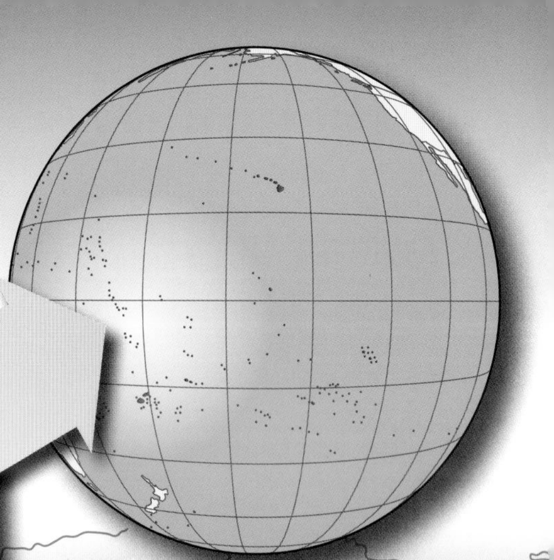

So much water.

From this side the world looks nearly all ocean. The **Pacific** is the biggest ocean.

1 See a bird of paradise.

The flag of **Papua New Guinea** shows the bird of paradise and 5 stars.

This way to Europe page 18

2 Life on an island.

Fishing is important. These people are trying to catch fish.

3 See a blue whale.

This the **biggest animal** that has ever lived!

RUSSIA
CHINA
NORTH KOREA
SOUTH KOREA
JAPAN
PAC
OC
TAIWAN
VIETNAM
PHILIPPINES
Micronesia
BRUNEI
MALAYSIA
PALAU
Melanesia
SINGAPORE
NAURU
KIR
INDONESIA
New Guinea
PAPUA NEW GUINEA
SOLOMON ISLANDS
TUVALU
EAST TIMOR
VANUATU
SAMC
FIJI
TON
AUSTRALIA
NEW ZEALAND
0 1,000 km 2,000 km 4,000 k

This way to Antarctica page 47

4 Let's look at a volcano.

Hawaii is part of the USA but it is a long way away. The islands are **volcanoes**.

5 Let's look under the sea.

This submarine takes people down deep under the ocean to see fish that swim there.

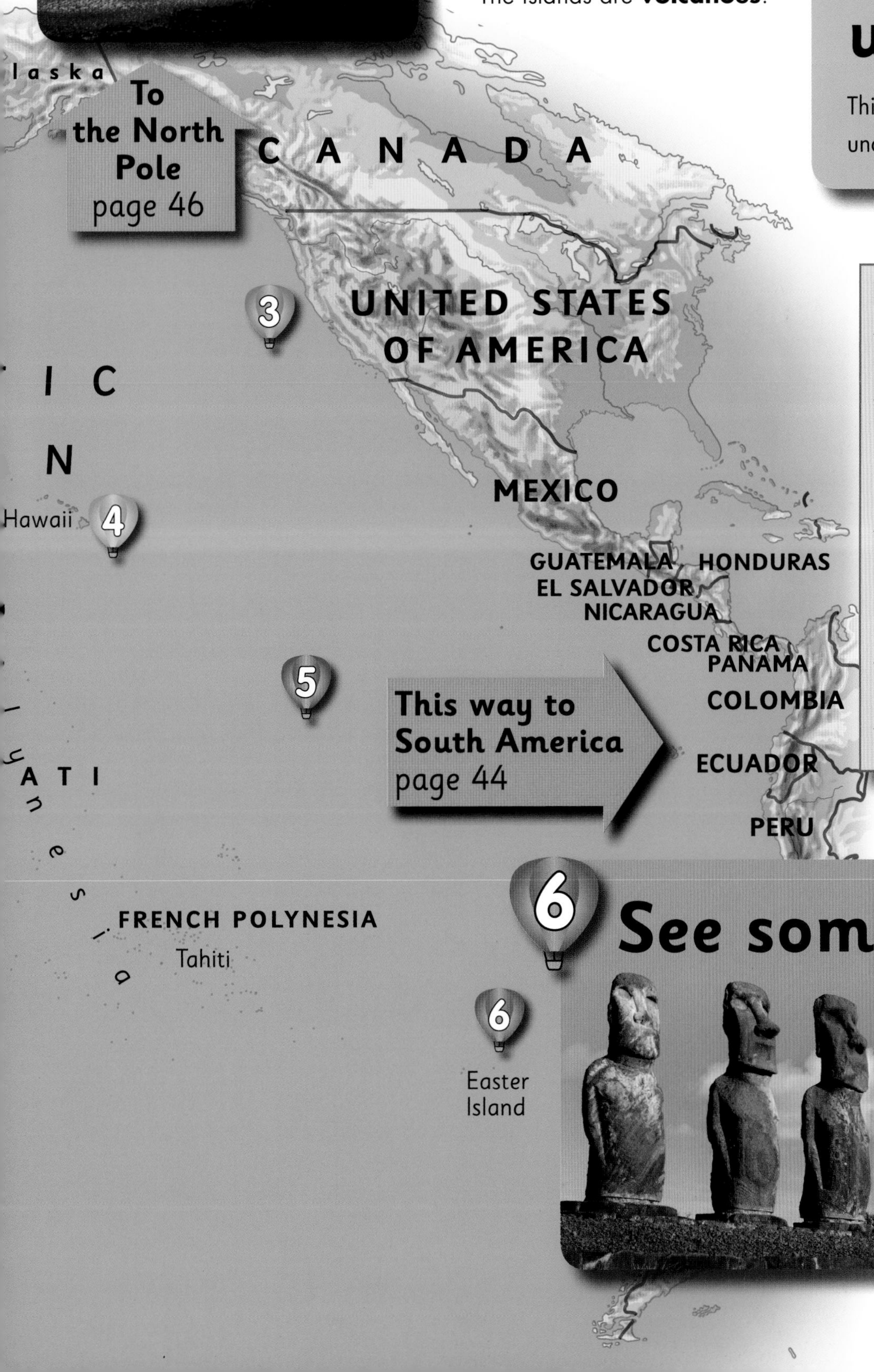

laska
CANADA
UNITED STATES OF AMERICA
3
I C
N
Hawaii
4
MEXICO
GUATEMALA
HONDURAS
EL SALVADOR
NICARAGUA
COSTA RICA
PANAMA
COLOMBIA
ECUADOR
PERU
5
A T I
FRENCH POLYNESIA
Tahiti
6
Easter Island

To the North Pole page 46

This way to South America page 44

Ideas for grown-ups

- ★ Talk about how big the Pacific is and how small the islands are.
- ★ Pacific islands are so far from other land that hardly any animals live here. But there are amazing birds and amazing sea creatures.
- ★ Talk about volcanoes. Volcanoes make land – most of the Pacific islands are there because of volcanoes, but not all the volcanoes are working.
- ★ Would you like to visit an island in the South Pacific?
- ★ Can you draw an Easter Island face?

6 See some big statues.

Long ago people on Easter Island made these amazing statues.

Find out about...

Australia and New Zealand

1 Crocodiles in Australia.

Salt water crocodiles are the biggest. They live where creeks (rivers) run out into the sea.

To Southeast Asia page 26

2 Paintings on the rock.

Aborigines have lived in Australia for a very long time – some paintings are very old. Can you see a fish?

3 Let's look for kangaroos.

Kangaroos live in **Australia**. They can jump over 9 metres in 1 jump! Can you see the baby 'roo' in mum's pouch?

This way to Antarctica page 47

A bridge and a city.

Sydney is the biggest city in Australia. This is the Sydney Harbour Bridge. Most people in Australia live near the sea.

A very old fern.

Trees like this **New Zealand** tree fern lived when the dinosaurs ruled the Earth!

This way to South America page 44

I am a kakapo.

Kakapos can't fly. They are very rare, but some are being kept safe on little islands.

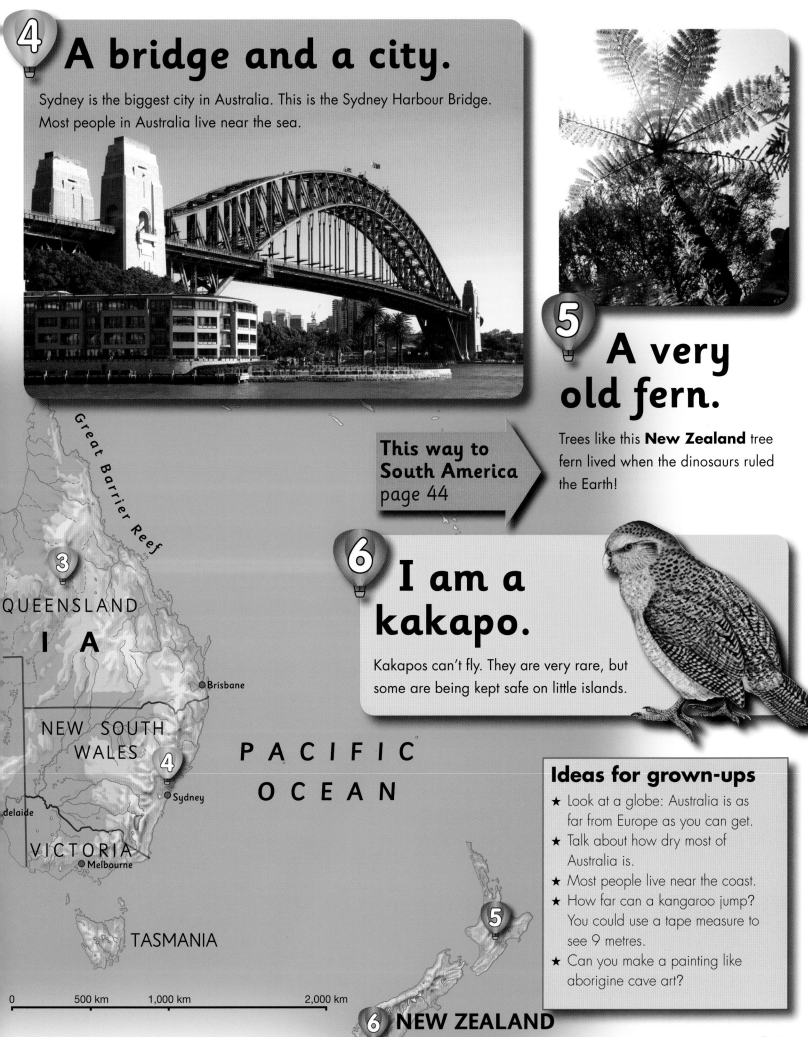

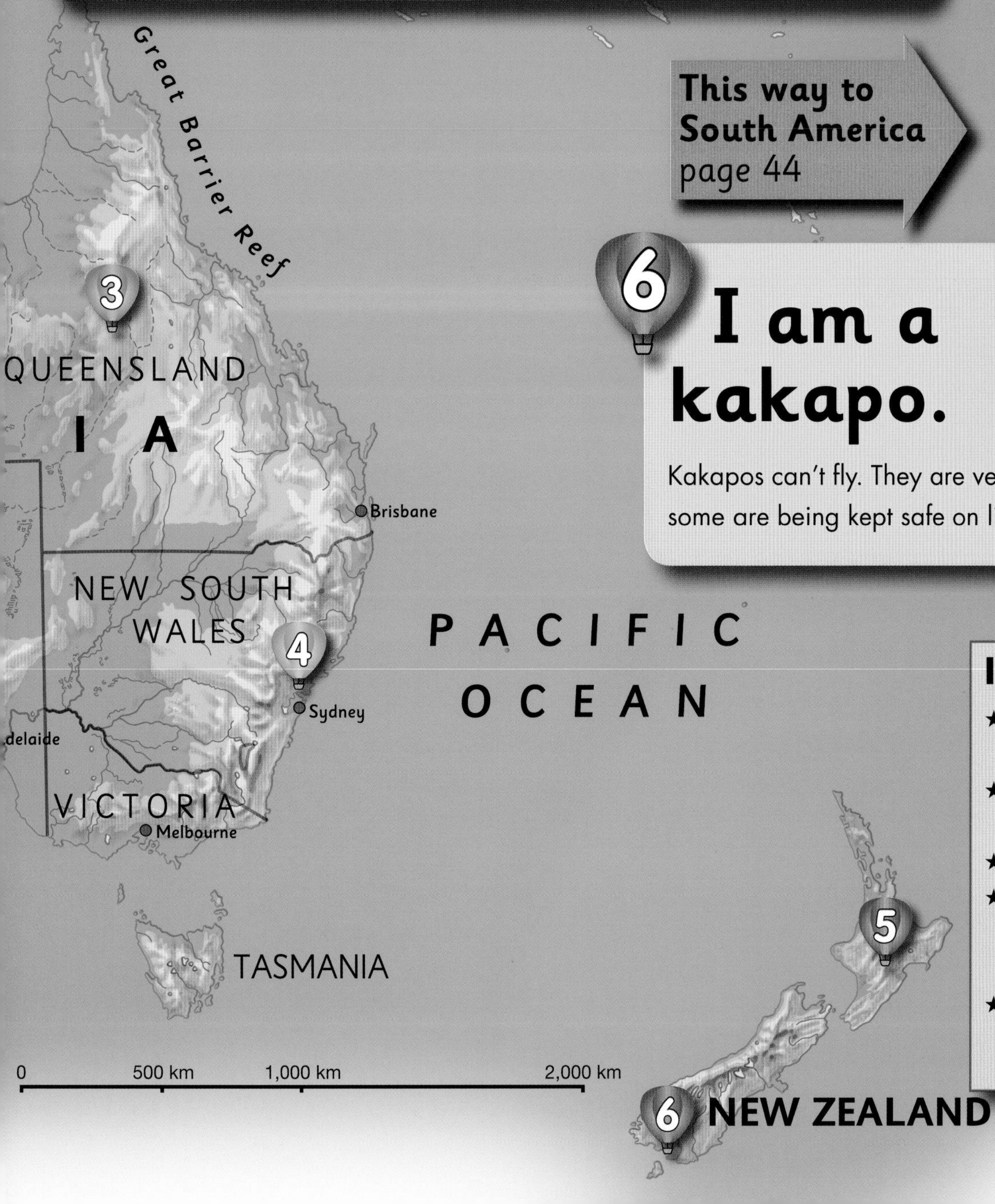
Great Barrier Reef
3
QUEENSLAND
Brisbane
NEW SOUTH WALES
4
Sydney
VICTORIA
Melbourne
TASMANIA
PACIFIC OCEAN
5
6
NEW ZEALAND
0
500 km
1,000 km
2,000 km

Ideas for grown-ups

- ★ Look at a globe: Australia is as far from Europe as you can get.
- ★ Talk about how dry most of Australia is.
- ★ Most people live near the coast.
- ★ How far can a kangaroo jump? You could use a tape measure to see 9 metres.
- ★ Can you make a painting like aborigine cave art?

Find out about...

Canada and Alaska

1 A big snowy mountain.

This is the highest mountain in North America. It is in **Alaska** which is part of the USA, so it is on a USA stamp.

80
USA
2001
Mount McKinley, Alaska

Ideas for grown-ups

- ★ Look at the globe for a route from the Pacific Ocean to the Arctic Ocean by sea. Have you found the Bering Strait? This route only works in summer. In winter it is closed by ice.
- ★ Talk about how COLD it is in winter! Even the Niagara Falls has icebergs!
- ★ Talk about flat land and mountains – what an amazing contrast!

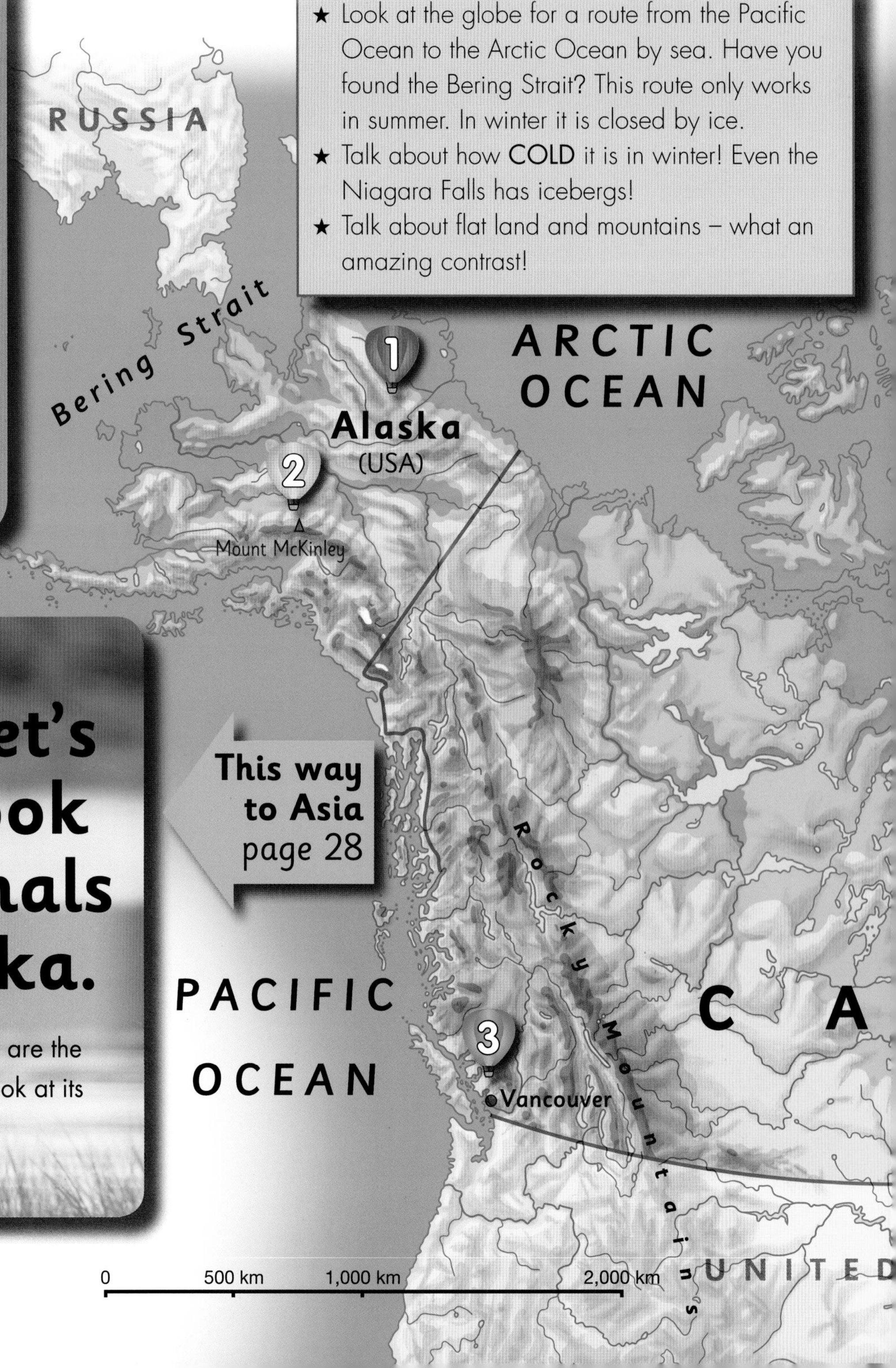

RUSSIA
Bering Strait
ARCTIC OCEAN
1
Alaska
(USA)
2
Mount McKinley
Rocky Mountains
PACIFIC OCEAN
3
Vancouver
C A
UNITED
0
500 km
1,000 km
2,000 km

This way to Asia page 28

2 Let's look at animals in Alaska.

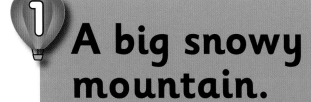

This is a **moose**. They are the biggest sort of deer. Look at its huge antlers.

3 Let's look at totem poles.

These totem poles in a park in Vancouver were carved from big trees by Native Americans. They tell stories in pictures.

4 Canada is cold in winter.

Winter in Canada is **very** cold – even colder than your freezer! The deep snow can be fun!

To the North Pole page 46

This way to Europe page 14

5 I can see red leaves.

The sap of the maple tree is sweet. **Maple syrup** is nice to pour on pancakes!

6 Trams in Toronto.

Good modern trams run in the streets of Toronto. Can you see the rails for the tram's wheels?

Find out about...
The USA

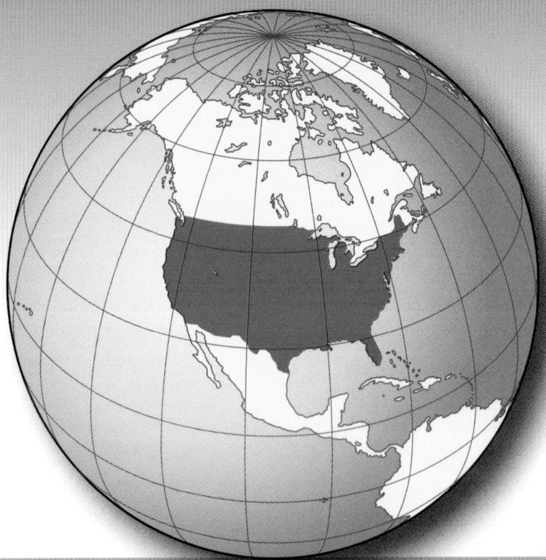

1 A city with tall buildings.

The tall buildings are called **skyscrapers**. Can you guess why? Can you see lots of cars on the highway? This city is called Seattle.

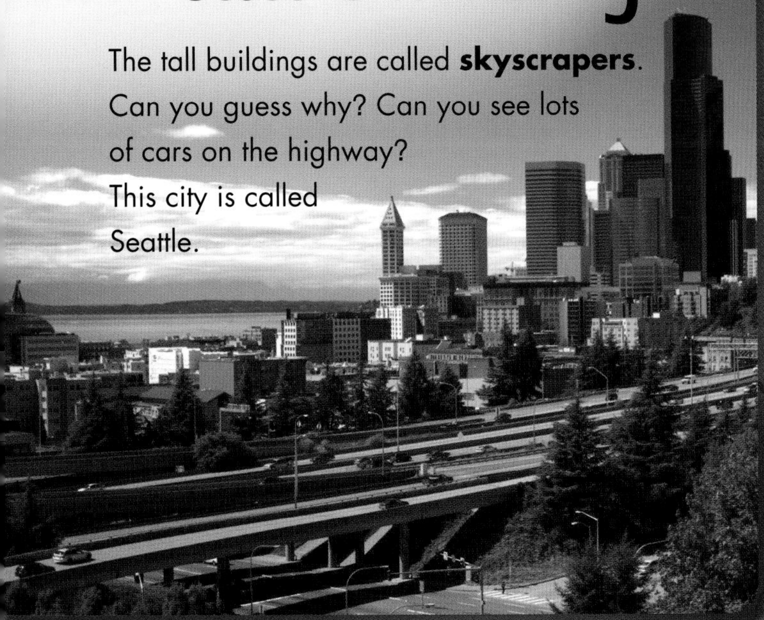

USA
20c
Cereus giganteus
Saguaro

3 Can you see a cactus?

Can you ... draw a cactus from the American desert? Remember don't touch – they are prickly.

2 A geyser in the USA.

Hot water whooshes out of the ground. It is called Old Faithful.

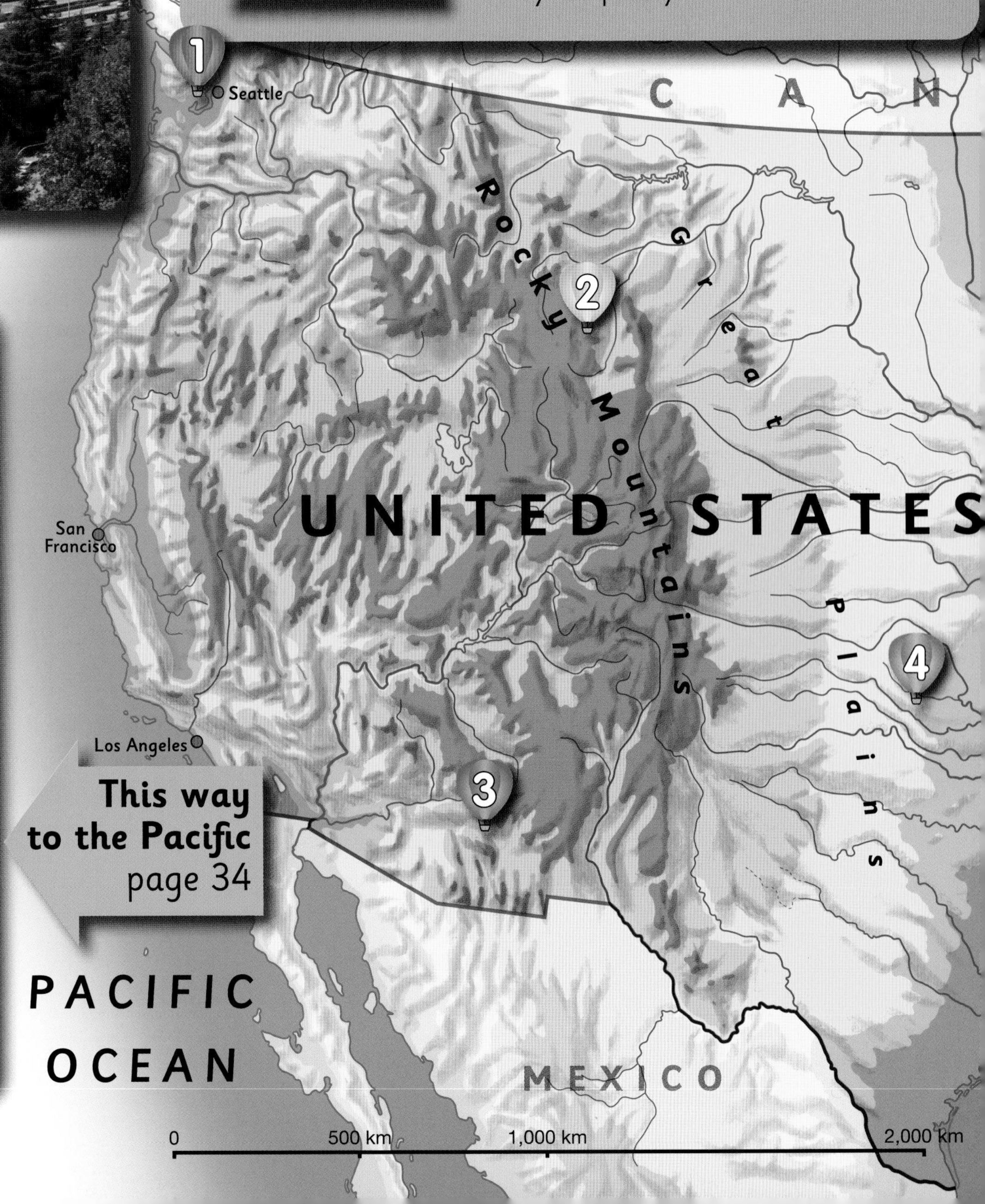
1
Seattle
CAN
Rocky Mountains
Great Plains
2
UNITED STATES
San Francisco
Los Angeles
3
4
PACIFIC OCEAN
MEXICO
0
500 km
1,000 km
2,000 km

This way to the Pacific page 34

4 Buffalo on the plains.

This is an American bison, but it is sometimes called a buffalo. There used to be millions of buffalo. Only a few are left but they are now protected.

5 I can see a rocket!

Lots of rockets take off from here. The Space Shuttle is launched from here – it is the only spacecraft that takes off, lands, and can be used again!

D
A
Lake Superior
Lake Michigan
Lake Huron
Lake Ontario
Lake Erie
Chicago
New York
F AMERICA
Appalachian Mts
Washington DC
6
Mississippi
New Orleans
ATLANTIC
OCEAN
5
Gulf of
Mexico
Miami

To Canada and Alaska page 38

This way to Europe page 14

To Central America page 42

Ideas for grown-ups

- ★ Explain USA means **U**nited **S**tates of **A**merica.
- ★ There are 50 states but two states are missing from this map. Can you find them? Find cold Alaska on page 38 (dress up warm!) and hot Hawaii on page 35 (beware of volcanoes!).
- ★ The flag of the USA has 50 stars. Can you guess why?
- ★ On the map, find the HIGH Rocky Mountains and the LOW land near the Mississippi River – where it sometimes floods.
- ★ Find the Great Lakes – are there 3 or **5** or 7?

6 Bears live in the forests.

22 USA
Black Bear

Black bears and brown bears (grizzly bears) live in America.

Find out about...

Central America

1 Let's visit a market.

Imagine you can ... **see** – all the different colours, **hear** – the people talking and shouting, **smell** – the spices, and **taste** – the juicy fruit.

3 Humming birds are tiny.

They can 'hover' by flapping their wings very fast.

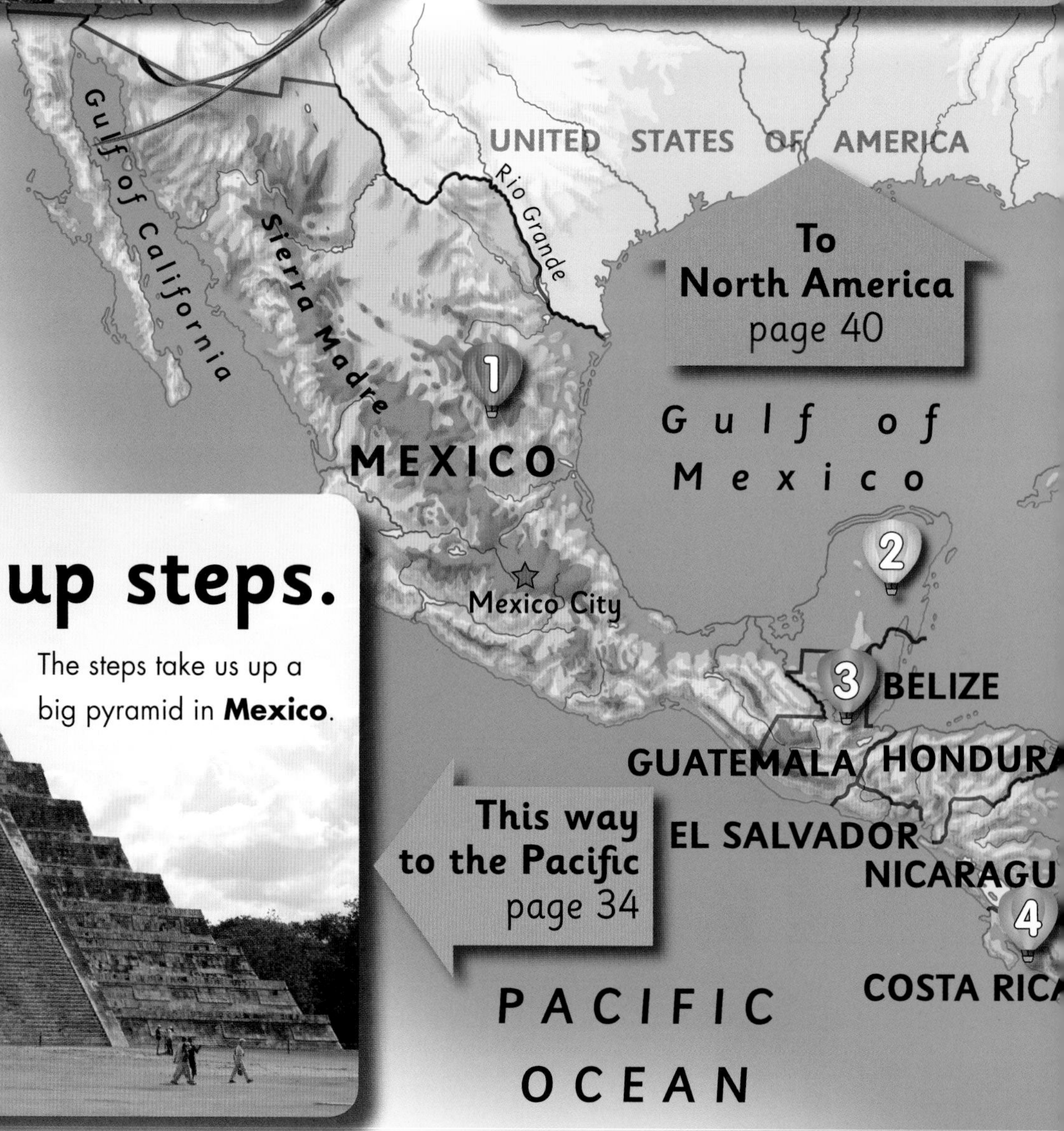
UNITED STATES OF AMERICA
Rio Grande
Gulf of California
Sierra Madre
1
MEXICO
Gulf of Mexico
2
Mexico City
3
BELIZE
GUATEMALA
HONDURA
EL SALVADOR
NICARAGU
4
COSTA RIC
PACIFIC OCEAN

To North America page 40

This way to the Pacific page 34

2 Let's climb up steps.

The steps take us up a big pyramid in **Mexico**.

4 Sloths live in the jungle.

They hang upside down from branches and move very slowly.

5 Fish in the sea.

Can you see the beautiful fragile **coral**? Lots of fish swim where coral lives.

This way to Africa page 30

To South America page 44

Ideas for grown-ups

Talk about:
What would you like to see? Mountains? Volcanoes? Seaside?

- ★ There are big cities too. Mexico City is one of the biggest.
- ★ Try some Mexican food – guacamole or tortillas!
- ★ Try moving slowly like a sloth and fast like a humming bird!
- ★ Talk about coral – how long it takes to grow and how important it is for sea creatures.

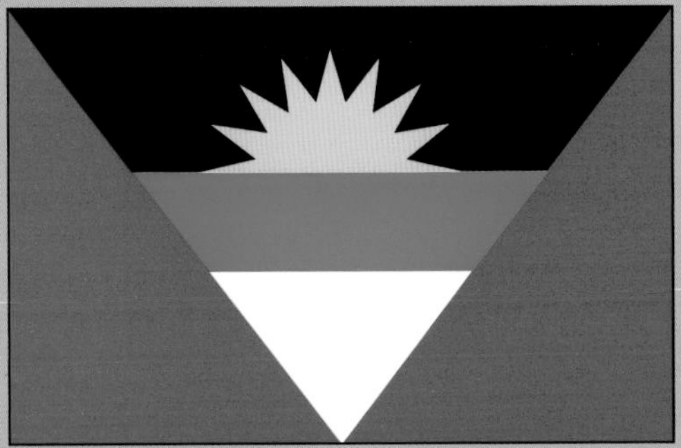

6 Can you see sun and sea?

This is the flag of **Antigua**. Blue = sea, white = coral beaches, gold = sunshine.

Find out about...

South America

To USA
page 40

This way
to the Pacific
page 34

1 A very long waterfall.

The highest waterfall in the world is called Angel Falls. It is in a country called **Venezuela**.

2 In the jungle of Brazil.

Lots of amazing animals live in the rainforest. The trees are so big. Some of the forest is being cut down. **Can you see** why the toucan is called the banana-beak bird?

Ideas for grown-ups

- ★ Enjoy the wild animals of South America.
- ★ Enjoy the map. Look at how big Brazil is. Can you count 10 countries that touch Brazil?
- ★ Build an Inca temple without cement. Use wooden building blocks. Would it last 600 years without glue?
- ★ Can you draw a llama?

This way to Africa
page 30

3 A big city in Brazil.

Brazil is the biggest country in South America. This is Rio de Janeiro: can you see skyscrapers, a crowded beach and amazing hills?

Amazing animals of South America.

Giant armadillos (left), anaconda snakes, jaguars, giant anteaters (right), piranha fish, giant tortoises, guinea pigs!

4 Super stones!

The huge stones of this **Inca temple** fit together so well they don't need cement. They are bigger than people and **llamas**! How did people cut and move them? No-one knows.

5 I am a real cowboy.

We look after the herds of cows that live on the big grasslands. In **Argentina** cowboys are called 'gauchos'.

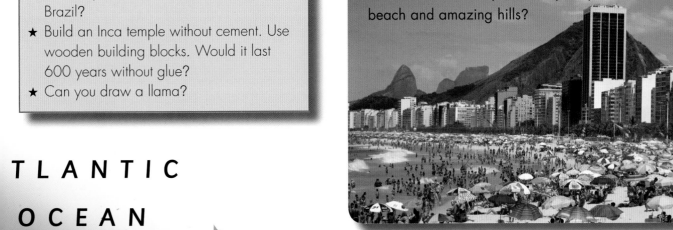

Find out about...
The Arctic

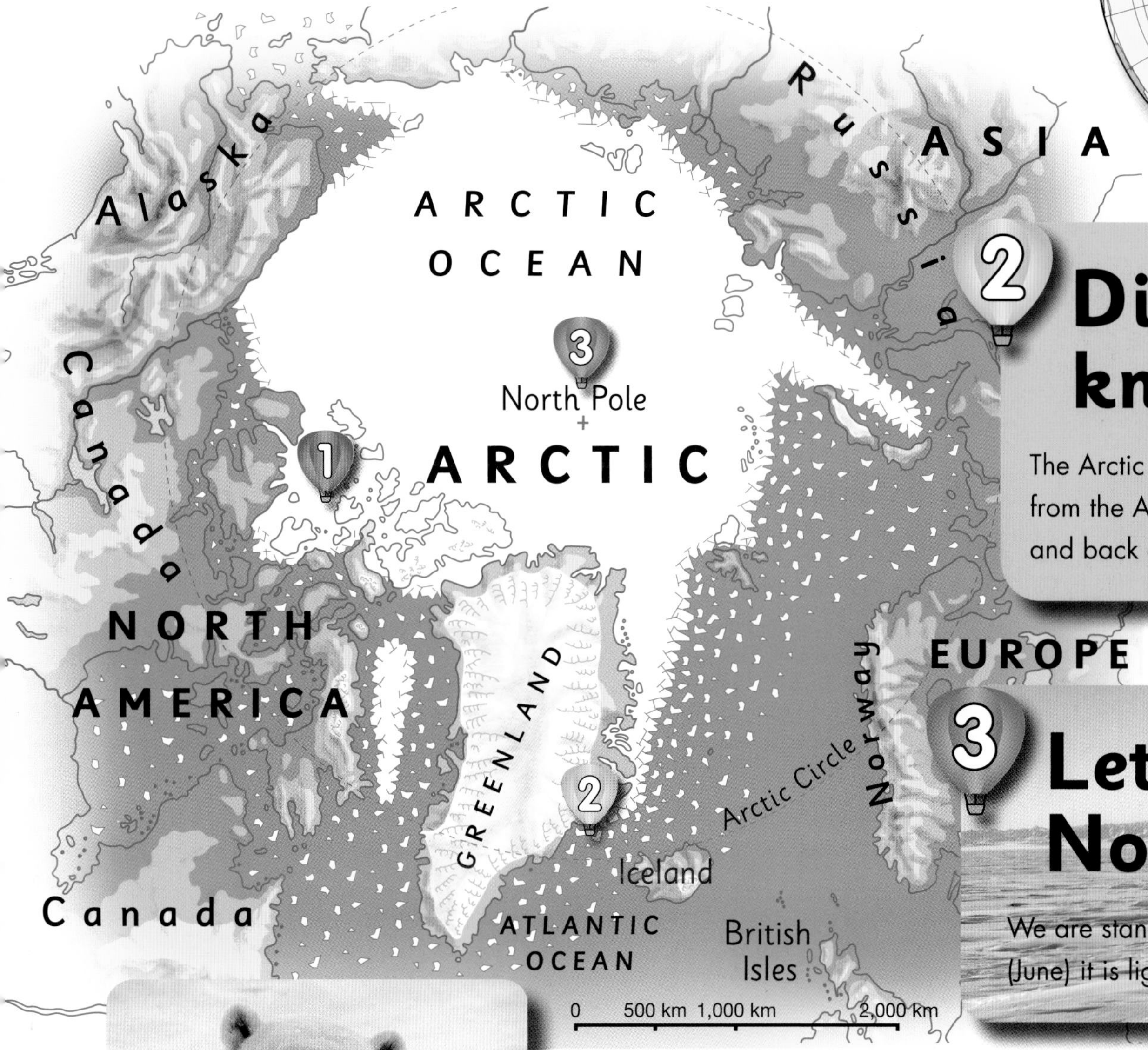
Alaska
Canada
Russia
ASIA
ARCTIC OCEAN
3
North Pole
1
ARCTIC
NORTH AMERICA
GREENLAND
2
Norway
EUROPE
Arctic Circle
Iceland
Canada
ATLANTIC OCEAN
British Isles
0 500 km 1,000 km 2,000 km

2 Did you know?

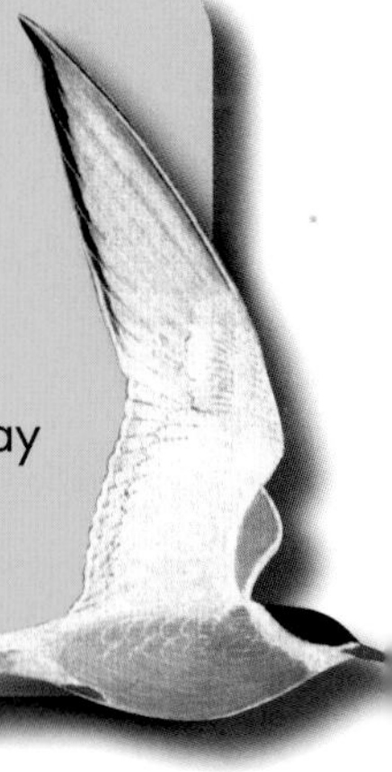

The Arctic tern flies all the way from the Arctic to Antarctica and back every year!

3 Let's go to the North Pole.

We are standing on frozen sea. In summer (June) it is light **all day** and **all night**.

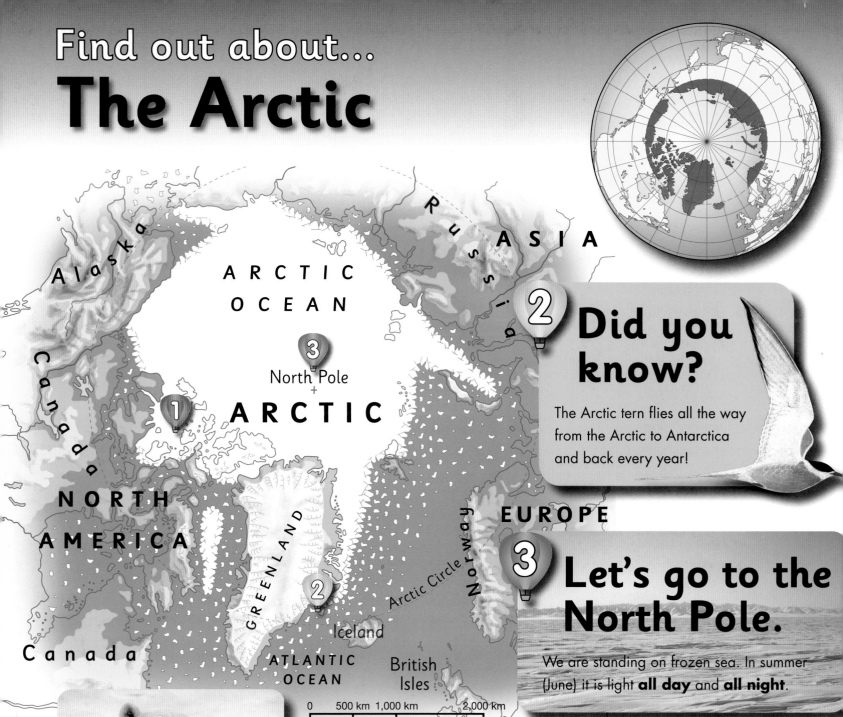

1 Let's find a polar bear.

Polar bears live in the Arctic. They are good swimmers. They eat seals and fish.

Ideas for grown-ups

Help the children to understand the maps by looking at a globe. White is ice: plain white is frozen sea, white with blue shadows is ice on land. Talk about:

- ★ The Arctic: There is a lot of land around the Arctic, but at the North Pole there is just frozen sea. No-one lives at the North Pole but people do live in the Arctic.
- ★ Antarctica: There is sea around Antarctica but at the South Pole there is land. Antarctica is the coldest, highest, most peaceful continent.
- ★ Can you make an iceberg? Float an ice cube in a cup – feel how cold it is. How much of it is under water?

Find out about...
Antarctica

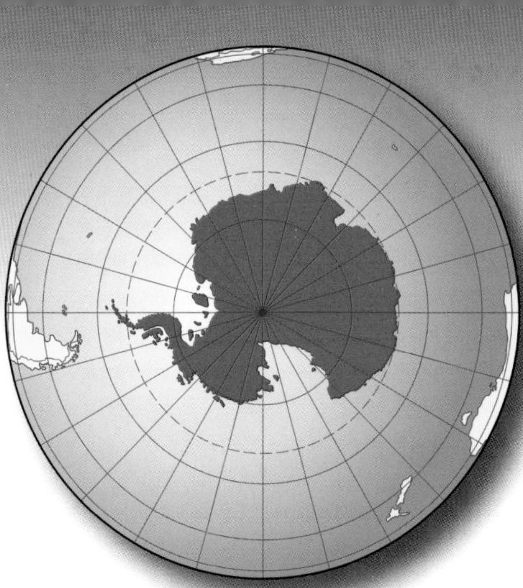

1 Let's look at icebergs.

In the summer some of the ice breaks off the ice sheet to make huge icebergs. The tourists in the boat must not get too close to the iceberg!

3 Let's look for people.

No-one lives on Antarctica, but scientists stay here. This scientist is finding out about the weather with a **balloon**.

4 Let's meet penguins.

5p
Adelie Penguin Pygoscelis adeliae
British Antarctic Territory

Penguins live in Antarctica. These are Adelie penguins. Can you see mum feeding the chick?

2 Let's look at seals.

Leopard seals live around Antarctica in the cold seas. They are good hunters just like leopards, but they are not as spotty!

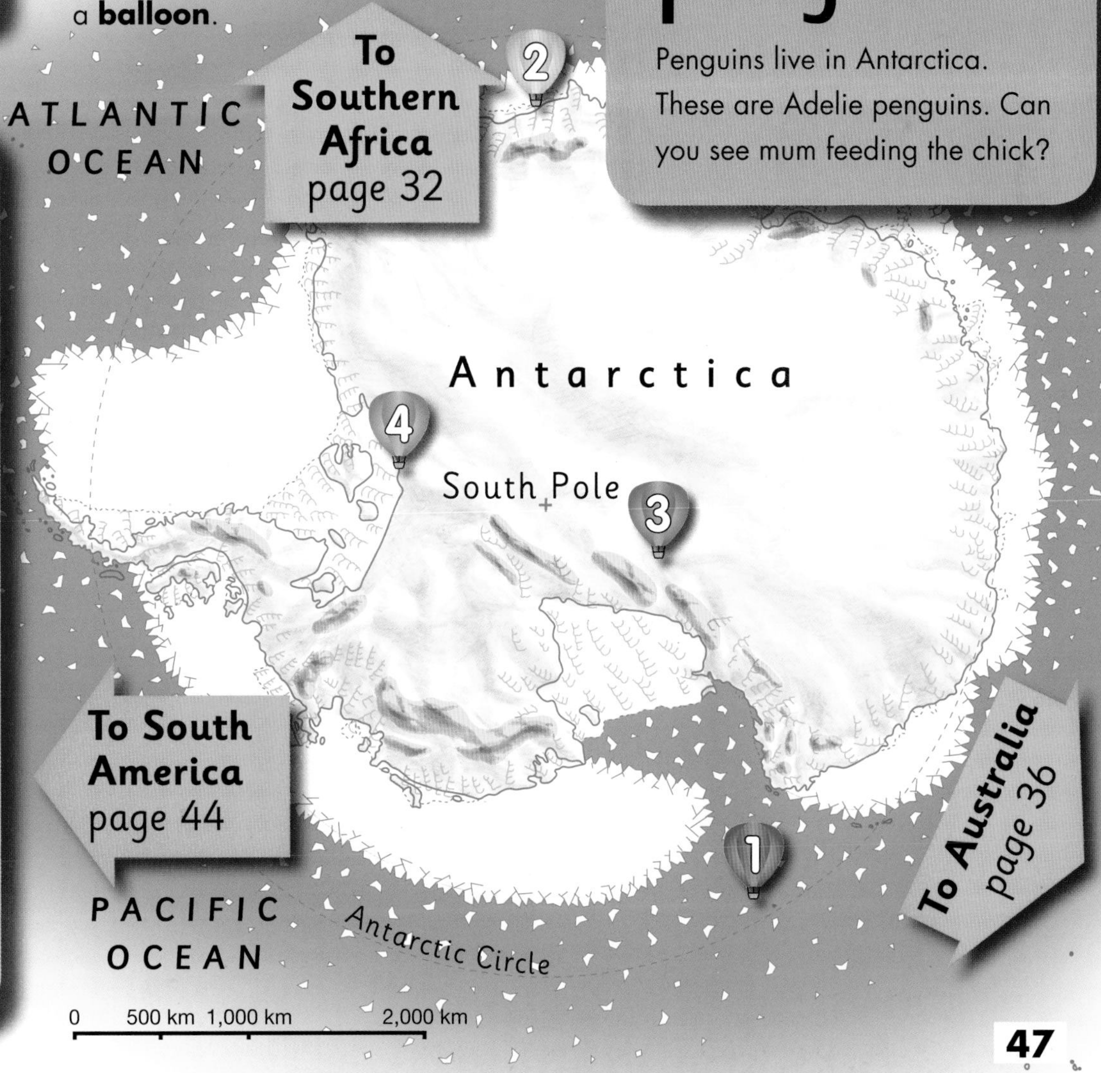
ATLANTIC OCEAN
To Southern Africa page 32
Antarctica
South Pole
To South America page 44
PACIFIC OCEAN
Antarctic Circle
To Australia page 36
0 500 km 1,000 km 2,000 km
1
2
3
4

Index of Places

Photo Acknowledgements

Alamy /Sarah Lawless 2 centre right, /Henry Westheim Photography 8 top, /Jon Arnold Images Ltd 8 upper centre, /imagebroker 8 lower centre, /imagebroker 8 bottom, /Jon Arnold Images Ltd 9 top left, /Motoring Picture Library 9 centre right, /Hideo Kurihara 12 bottom, /TravelStockCollection – Homer Sykes 15 bottom, /vario images GmbH & Co.KG 18 top left, /Juniors Bildarchiv 19 bottom right, /GoGo Images Corporation 29 top left, /Jason Gallier 30 bottom left, /marcus wilson-smith 32 top left, /Dave Marsden 37 top right, /Dorothy Keeler 38 bottom, /Design Pics Inc. 39 top right, /culliganphoto 39 bottom, /imagebroker 42 top left, /Peter Adams Photography Ltd 45 bottom right; **Corbis** /JLP/Jose L. Pelaez 6 bottom, /The Irish Image Collection 13 top, /Tim Thompson 13 centre, /Steven Vidler/Eurasia Press 14 centre left, /Hulton-Deutsch Collection 16 top left, /S. Carmona 17 top right, /Tom Brakefield 20 top left, /David Turnley 20 top right, /Wolfgang Kaehler 21 top left, /Richard T. Nowitz 23 top, /Reuters 23 bottom, /Galen Rowell 24 centre left, /Reuters 25 top right, /Sukree Sukplang/Reuters 26 centre, /Theo Allofs 27 top right, /NAOAKI WATANABE/amanaimages 29 bottom, /Jose Fuste Raga 30 top left, /James Marshall 31 top, /Tom Grill 33 centre, /Patrick Frilet/Hemis 34 centre left, /Douglas Peebles 35 top left, /Joel W. Rogers 39 top left, /Lester Lefkowitz 40 bottom, /Ralph A. Clevinger (RF) 43 top left (background), /Stuart Westmorland 43 top right, /Frans Lemmens/zefa 45 bottom left, /Richard Wear/Design Pics 47 top left, /Graham Neden/Ecoscene 47 top centre; **DeepSeaPhotography.Com** /Peter Batson 35 top right; **Dreamstime.com** /Sebcz 10, /Lesscholz 14 bottom, /Tebnad 15 top right, /Mayangsari 16 top right, /Garnham123 17 top left, /Tugores34 17 bottom, /Olexa 18 bottom, /Yuri4u80 19 top, /Costa007 19 bottom left (background), /Skynesher 34 bottom right (background), /Freezingpictures 47 bottom; **Fotolia.com** /Xenia1972 9 top right, /Alan Bishop 27 top left, /Celso Pupo 45 top; **iStockphoto.com** /SVLumagraphica 11, /Andresr 12 top left, /Rob Broek 13 bottom, /Mark Harris 14 top left, /Bogdan Boghitoi 19 centre, /vera bogaerts 22 top left, /Ewen Cameron 25 top left, /Emma Holmwood 25 bottom, /Nikolai Zauber 26 bottom, /Chris Ronneseth 28 centre, /Christophe Testi 29 top right, /Csaba Tóth 31 bottom, /Adam Kuert 32 bottom, /Wolfgang Steiner 33 top right, /Jan Rihak 35 bottom, /DHuss 36 centre, /Phillip Minnis 37 top left, /Gavin Jung 39 centre, /Rick Hyman 40 top left, /Oleg Albinsky 42 bottom, /Birgit Prentner 44 top left, /Brasil2 44 bottom left, /Max Lindenthaler 46 centre right, /John Pitcher 46 bottom; **NASA** /4, 5, 41 top right; **saudiaramco.com** /22 bottom.

Picture Glossary: exciting 'world words'

Ideas for grown-ups

These pictures and words will help to develop our 'Knowledge and Understanding of the World'. Choose a topic that interests us today – find the page number beside the word, and you can find a full-size picture with some information about it.

Country flags from around the World

Lebanon | Lesotho | Liberia | Libya | Liechtenstein | Lithuania | Luxembou

Marshall Islands | Mauritania | Mauritius | Mexico | Micronesia | Moldova | Monaco

Netherlands | New Zealand | Nicaragua | Niger | Nigeria | Northern Marianas | Norway

Poland | Portugal | Puerto Rico | Qatar | Romania | Russia | Rwanda

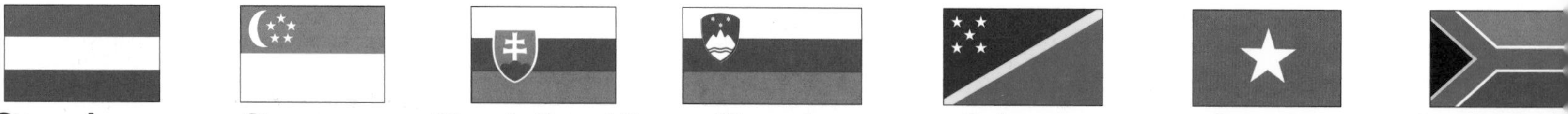

Sierra Leone | Singapore | Slovak Republic | Slovenia | Solomon Islands | Somalia | South Afri

Swaziland | Sweden | Switzerland | Syria | Taiwan | Tajikistan | Tanzania

Tuvalu | Uganda | Ukraine | United Arab Emirates | United Kingdom | United States of America | Uruguay